THE INTERNATIONAL OPERATIONS OF NATIONAL FIRMS:
A STUDY OF DIRECT FOREIGN INVESTMENT

M. I. T. MONOGRAPHS IN ECONOMICS

THE INTERNATIONAL OPERATIONS OF NATIONAL FIRMS: A STUDY OF DIRECT FOREIGN INVESTMENT

Stephen Herbert Hymer

The MIT Press
Cambridge, Massachusetts, and London, England

This book was typed on IBM Executive by Inge Calci,
and printed and bound in the United States of America.

Second printing, 1977

Library of Congress Cataloging in Publication Data

Hymer, Stephen.
    The international operations of national firms.

    (M. I. T. monographs in economics; 14)
    Originally presented as the author's thesis,
Massachusetts Institute of Technology, 1960.
    Vita.
    Bibliography: p.
    Includes index.
    1. International business enterprises.
2. Investments, foreign. 3. Investments, American.
4. Corporations, American. I. Title. II. Series.
HD69.I7H94   1976   338.8'8   75-33365
ISBN 0-262-08085-0

CONTENTS

Contents

Contents

TABLES

INTRODUCTION

Stephen H. Hymer was killed in an automobile accident on February 4, 1974, cutting short at the age of thirty-nine a brilliant and eventful career in economics. He had received a B.A. with first-class honors in economics and political science at McGill University in his native Montreal in 1955 and came to M.I.T. in the fall of that year to study industrial relations. Over time, his interests shifted to economic theory, industrial organization, and international trade. The last two fields were combined in his doctoral dissertation, completed in 1960, and now finally published.

In 1960, the Department of Economics at M.I.T. had already begun the practice of publishing, with subvention and by means of The M.I.T. Press, certain theses of outstanding merit. A number of theses, of course, found outside publishers, but the departmental series was considered to have a certain prestige. Hymer's dissertation was submitted for publication in the departmental series by me but was rejected. It was stated by one member of the selection committee that the argument was too simple and straightforward. My reply did not move the committee: that to make clear a field in which theory had long been confused was a first-class contribution to scholarship. Now, fifteen

years later, the committee has reversed its early position.

The penetrating insights of the thesis into the nature
of direct investment nevertheless found their way into
economic analysis. The second and third editions of
my textbook International Economics used Hymer's
approach and called attention to the existence of the
thesis. By the mid-1960s, Hymer was publishing material in the periodical literature on the subject. That
writing, and the attention drawn to the thesis in various ways, brought it a notoriety, if that is the right
word, and an underground existence. Interlibrary
loans of it flourished, and the Xerox Company waxed
rich on its reproduction. In due time, Stephen Hymer
was approached by the economics editor of a major
international university press on whether he would be
willing to have the thesis published ten years after its
completion. He agreed but wanted to make some changes.
By the time of his death three or so years later, there
was no indication of how he would have changed it. This
text is identical with that submitted for the degree in
1960, with minimal editorial corrections. Since the
contribution lies in the economic analysis, obsolescence
of the data does not constitute a drawback.

Outstanding theses that are never published are rare,
much rarer than the contrary, the mediocre contribu-
tions that do appear in letterpress and hard covers. A
number of significant theses have been long delayed,
especially Alec Cairncross's 1939 dissertation Home
and Foreign Investment, 1870-1913 (Cambridge:
Cambridge University Press, 1953), the revision of
which was interrupted by World War II. One famous
thesis, widely studied in the London School of Economics, is J. B. Jeffrys's "Trends in Business Organization since 1856," submitted in 1938 and not published for many reasons, including, I am told, the in-
terruption caused by the war, political differences
among some of the principals, and Dr. Jeffrys's de-
parture from academic life for business. I know of only
one other posthumously published thesis, Charles Ballot's Introduction du machinisme dans l'industrie
francaise (Paris: Rieder, 1923), which has in parentheses after the name of the author another name, that
of Claude Gevel, who headed the team of Ballot's friends
who wrote the thesis from his notes after Ballot was
killed in World War I.

This is not the only posthumously published work
from the pen of Stephen Hymer. Collections of his es-

says have already appeared in Italian, Japanese, and
Spanish, and a group of his friends and colleagues are
arranging to bring them out in an American edition.
These friends have formed the Stephen Hymer Papers
Collective, and they are associated, as he was in the
last years of his life, with the Union for Radical Political Economics.

About 1966 or 1967, it became clear that Stephen
Hymer had been changing his views. By 1969, he pub-
licly announced that he was personally commited to
Marxism and to radical changes in this society. When
he moved from Yale to the New School for Social Research in 1970, he was instrumental in launching a new
program in political economy within the Department of
Economics.

It would be futile to conjecture on the forces that
brought about this change of perspective. From M.I.T.,
Hymer went to Ghana to study economic development as
an employee, if my memory serves, of the Ghanaian
Planning Board under the Nkrumah government. There
began an interest in developing countries, unrelated at
the time to the presence of the multinational corporation, and focused more fully on the response to market
prices of native African farmers producing cocoa.

Later on, at Yale, he continued to work on Ghana, as
well as international business, and ultimately published,
alone and in collaboration, some eight papers, out of
about fifty written, on topics of Africa and economic
development.

From Ghana, Hymer returned to M. I. T. in 1962 as
an assistant professor for one year. The Department
of Economics normally is unwilling to hire its own
graduates, but in this case, it generously enabled
Hymer to reenter the job market for economists in the
United States, which was virtually impossible to accomplish from Accra. I had supervised his thesis from
1958 to 1960 and worked closely with him again that
year. We became fast friends and remained so after
he left in the fall of 1962 to join the Economic Growth
Center and the Department of Economics of Yale University.

In 1961-1962 and again at Yale in the following years,
Hymer tried to distill the gist of his thesis into a single
definitive article and failed to get that published. My
files are at best chaotic, but they contain a fascinating
letter, dated 1966, recounting the rejection of his ef-
forts by the American Economic Review and the Journal
of Political Economy, with extensive comments by the

referees and in one case an editor. He had already
broken into print in 1962 with two joint articles, written as a graduate student with his fellow student B.
Peter Pashigian, on subjects in industrial organization.
Later he would frequently write with a collaborator (ten
of his papers are collaborations). As one who was emo-
tionally involved in his success at this time, I am not
in a position to judge whether the referees and editors
were right or wrong in rejecting the draft article "International Firms and International Capital Markets,"
or whether at that time he was afflicted by a real "block"
to creative scholarship of the sort widely known in academic life. In conversation he was highly prolific with
ideas at this time and published on less general themes,
especially in collaboration. He did feel a sense of frus-
tration, however, at being unable to get the major contribution embodied in his thesis into print.

Hymer's radical viewpoint was not, I believe, developed in Ghana, and its origins at a later date are
not clear to me. His sabbatical in 1968-1969 took him
to Cambridge, England, where he worked with Robert
Rowthorn, a Marxist economist; to the University of
the West Indies in Jamaica, where he saw direct investment from the point of view of the host country;

and to Chile, where he studied the operations of American copper companies. Whatever the reasons for his
shift to radical economics, Hymer began writing more
at this time, and his ideas seemed to flow. He became
widely known outside the United States. Maurice Byé,
an early and neglected pioneer of la grande entreprise
multinationale,[1] asked him to contribute to a symposium. With Rowthorn he wrote for a symposium on The
International Corporation, which I edited (Cambridge,
Mass.: M.I.T. Press, 1970), and with Stephen Resnick
in a collection, edited by Jagdish Bhagwati, Ronald W.
Jones, Robert Mundell, and Jaroslav Vanek, entitled
Trade, Balance of Payments and Growth (Amsterdam:
North Holland Publishing Company, 1971).

His influence extended beyond scholarly publication.
It was in the spring of 1967, I believe, that I ran into
him and another Canadian M.I.T. graduate student in
economics, Melville Watkins, at a seminar at the University of Toronto. Hymer was working with Watkins

[1] See Maurice Byé, "Self-Financed Multiterritorial Units
and Their Time Horizon," in International Economic Association, International Economic Papers, No. 8 (New
York: The Macmillan Company, 1958; original French
version dated 1957).

on the highly nationalistic "Watkins Report."[2] I recall
thinking that Hymer had had a strong influence on the
tone of the report. When I asked why they recommended
national instead of international action to curb the multinational, largely United States, corporations operating
in Canada, it was Hymer who replied that Canada always called for international rather than national action and that this was a cop-out because international
action of sufficient power and restraint was impossible
to achieve.

In 1967-1968, when I was spending the year in Atlanta,
Georgia, Stephen Hymer volunteered to pay me a visit
to see firsthand the problems of black education. I arranged for Hymer to give a seminar on the multinational corporation at Georgia State University, and I
still retain a vivid impression of the force and bril-
liance of his economic analysis, then rapidly turning
to the left. I also have a lively recollection of his participation in the first independent Union for Radical
Political Economics convention in New York in Decem-

---

[2] Foreign Ownership and the Structure of Canadian In-
dustry, Report of the Task Force on the Structure of
Canadian Industry, prepared for the Privy Council
(Ottawa: Queen's Printer, January 1968).

ber 1969, parallel to that of the American Economic
Association. Stephen Hymer stood with his fellow radi-
cals when they marched into the business meeting and
demanded action on several militant resolutions, but
he did not participate in the disorder. I think it was in
the spring of 1973, under the auspices of the Graduate
Student Association at M. I. T., that Robert Stobaugh
and I debated Hymer and Watkins on a question whose
phraseology I do not recall, but which was basically
on whether multinational corporations are good or evil.
The audience was so large that the usual seminar room
had to be abandoned for an auditorium. The debate was
spirited, even sharp, but warm and friendly. A few
days after Hymer's death, I participated on a panel to
discuss the same subject at the United Nations Staff
Club in New York, where mainstream and radical points
of view were joined in a vigorous clash. Stephen Hymer
had intended to be there to help Paul Sweezy, Harry
Magdoff, and others challenge me. I missed him and
still miss him deeply.

This account of Stephen Hymer's political and economic views, as they evolved over the years, has perhaps little to do with his thesis, but it indicates at
least that any mainstream value judgments that may

be detected in the analysis of his thesis had been sub-
sequently modified. I regard the analysis as neutral,
cutting both for and against the multinational corporation and arming with better understanding both its de-
fenders and its attackers. To understand is not always
to forgive. It is necessary, however, to understand.
The Department of Economics is thus proud to present
the early, unpolished, once-rejected thesis of Stephen
H. Hymer, Ph.D., M.I.T., 1960, as an important
contribution to the history of economic thought.

Charles P. Kindleberger
Cambridge, Massachusetts, May 1975

THE INTERNATIONAL OPERATIONS OF
NATIONAL FIRMS:
A STUDY OF DIRECT FOREIGN INVESTMENT

A COMPARISON OF DIRECT AND PORTFOLIO INVESTMENT

The Definitions of Direct and Portfolio Investment and Some Empirical Evidence of Differences in Their Behavior

It is customary to distinguish two kinds of long-term private international capital movements—direct investment and portfolio investment. Not everyone makes the distinction in quite the same way, but there is a great deal of similarity, and basically it is a question of who controls the enterprise in which the investment is made. If the investor directly controls the foreign enterprise, his investment is called a direct investment. If he does not control it, his investment is a portfolio investment.

Control is not an easy thing to define, and the dividing line between some control and no control is arbitrary. The United States Department of Commerce, for example, considers a foreign enterprise to be American-controlled if it is wholly owned, as in the case of a branch plant, or if 25 percent of the equity is held by an American or group of affiliated Americans, of if 50 percent of the equity is held by Americans even though no single group has 25 percent. If, by this definition, the enterprise is deemed to be American-controlled, all American investment in that enterprise is

classified as direct investment. All other investment,
that is, investment in corporations not controlled by
Americans or investment in foreign government bonds
is classified as portfolio investment.[1]

The details of the definition are not important. We
are concerned with why this distinction is made at all.
Whatever the theory behind the distinction, the facts,
at least, seem to support its usefulness. Direct investment, as defined here, has behaved quite differently from portfolio investment, and this suggests that
they really are two different things. The most striking
example of this difference in behavior is found in the
changes in the United States long-term investment position since 1914.

The trend of United States long-term investments in
the present century is shown in Table 1.1. Four points
which illustrate the differences and similarities in the
behavior of direct and portfolio investment may be
noted.

[1] U.S. Department of Commerce, Office of Business
Economics, Direct Private Foreign Investments of the
United States: Census of 1950 (Washington: U.S. Gov-
ernment Printing Office, 1953), pp. 4, 37.

Table 1.1 United States Direct and Portfolio Investment Position in Selected Years, 1914-1956 (billions of dollars)

	1914	1919	1930	1939	1946	1956
United States investments abroad						
Direct investments	2.6	3.9	8.0	7.0	7.2	22.1
Portfolio investments	.9	2.6	7.2	3.8	5.1	7.9
Foreign investments in the United States						
Direct investments	1.3	.9	1.4	2.0	2.5	4.5
Portfolio investments	5.4	2.3	4.3	4.3	4.5	8.8

Sources: 1914-1946. S. Pizer and F. Cutler, "Growth of Foreign Investments in the United States and Abroad." Survey of Current Business, XXXVI (August 1956), p. 15.

1956. U.S. Department of Commerce, Office of Business Economics, Balance of Payments: Statistical Supplement (Washington: U.S. Government Printing Office, 1958), p. 181.

1. By 1914 the United States had substantial direct investment but hardly any portfolio investment. In fact, at that time, the United States was a recipient of large amounts of portfolio investment.

2. In the twenties, direct and portfolio investment moved in a similar fashion, both expanding rapidly.

3. In the thirties, while portfolio investments declined drastically, direct investments declined only slightly.

4. In the postwar period, there was a rapid expansion
of direct investment but only a slight increase in portfolio. It is significant that during this period, portfolio
funds flew into the United States.

So much for the historical trend. There are also
some important differences in the area distribution
shown in Table 1.2. In 1929 the United States had about
the same amount of direct investment as portfolio investment: $7.5 billion in the case of direct and $8.1
billion of portfolio investments. In Canada, portfolio
investment exceeded direct investment somewhat. In
Europe there was almost two and one half times as
much portfolio investment as there was direct. In
Latin America the ratio was reversed. The 1956 data
also show differences in the distribution of the two
kinds of investments.

More statistical evidence on the difference in behavior between portfolio and direct investment could
be offered, but at this point it would hardly serve any
purpose. A perfectly arbitrary twofold classification
of capital movements could also show differences in
behavior and most probably would. The point is to show
that there are theoretical differences which account
for the discrepancy in behavior. This is a large order,

Table 1.2 United States Direct and Portfolio Investments
Abroad by Area, 1929 and 1956 (billions of dollars)

	1929		1956	
Area	Direct Investment	Portfolio Investment	Direct Investment	Portfolio Investment
Canada	1.7	2.0	7.5	4.3
Europe	1.3	3.5	3.5	1.7
Latin America	3.7	1.7	7.4	.8
Other	.7	1.0	3.7	1.2[a]
Totals[b]	7.4[c]	8.1	22.1	7.9

[a]International institutions accounted for .4 of this amount.

[b]Totals may not add because of rounding.

[c]Does not include direct investment of .1 in banking.
Sources: 1929. C. Lewis, America's Stake in International Investments (Washington: The Brookings Institution, 1938), pp. 606, 654.

1956. U.S. Department of Commerce, Office of Business Economics, Balance of Payments: Statistical Supplement, p. 181.

and what we try to accomplish is considerably less
ambitious. We begin with a discussion of the theory of
portfolio capital movements and then try to apply this
theory to direct investment.

The Theory of Portfolio Investment

For portfolio investment, a well-developed theory exists. It is worthwhile considering it in detail, for it
has many similarities and contrasts with the explanation of direct investment which will be offered. Although we shall reject the theory as the explanation of
direct investment, we shall later need many of the considerations dealt with here.

The basis of the theory of portfolio investment is the
interest rate. Each investor maximizes his profits by
investing where returns are the highest. Under the
simplest form of the theory—where there are no risks,
uncertainties, or barriers to movement—capital will
move from countries where the interest rate is low to
countries where it is high until interest rates are
everywhere equal. In this simple case, the theory
predicts that no cross movements of capital will occur.

The theory in this simplest form is too naive. The
difficulty is that when risk, uncertainty, and barriers

to movement are introduced, almost anything can happen. The extra empirical information needed to make
predictions is very great and almost impossible to acquire.

If risk is introduced, the equilibrium condition is
that equities of equal risk and equal return sell at the
same price. We can now no longer easily predict the
direction of the capital flow. In fact, cross movements
are likely to occur on two accounts. They will occur,
first of all, because of differences in risk preference.
If the investors of one country are more conservative
on the average than the rest of the world, risk-avoid-
ing capital will flow out of the country, while risk-
taking capital will flow in. Even if risk preferences
are the same, cross movements will occur because
of the desire of investors to diversify. As a corollary,
this means that the interest costs on a loan will be
greater for a larger loan even if the risk on the project, as defined, for example, by the standard devia-
tion of the expected returns, is the same as for a
smaller loan. The reason is as follows: the more
people invest in a particular project, the less diversi-
fied their portfolio becomes. To make up for the increased risk caused by this loss of diversification, a

higher interest rate must be offered. This may be an important factor in international capital flows, for most international investment was and is concerned with large projects. It may be that these large projects can be financed only in large capital markets, where there are many investors, each willing and able to take a small part. This cause rather than interest rates in general might then account for some or much of international capital movements.

If we introduce uncertainty, so that there is disagreement about what risk is involved in a given security, then cross movements will also occur merely as a result of differences in evaluation.

Even now, the task of empirical verification is indeed considerable. But there are further complications, since we have not yet taken into account barriers to movement and imperfections in the market. The main barrier to movement, aside from government control, is the possibility of changes in the exchange rate. If the future exchange rate is uncertain, then returns to an investment in a given country are not the same for natives as for foreigners. The foreigner must consider the exchange rate he will get or, more correctly, the probability distribution of future exchange rates.

When he enters this into his calculations, it might either decrease or increase the risk involved. If it increases the risk, this is an additional cost. The cost might very well work in both directions, and it is therefore similar in principle to transport costs. Investors in each country might, for example, consider a 4 percent return abroad as equivalent to a 3 percent return at home because of exchange risk. The main point is that equilibrium does not require equalization of interest rates throughout the world. The only necessary equilibrium condition is that interest rates in any two countries should not differ by more than a certain amount. Fluctuations in the interest rates can occur without eliciting capital movements unless the fluctuations are sufficiently large.

Something similar happens when there are other barriers to movement, such as the high costs of acquiring information or of making transactions. Then, equivalent securities in different countries can sell at different rates because the discrepancy is not known or because the cost of removing it is too great.

The theory of portfolio investment with all the complications introduced does not provide clear-cut answers to the question of which way capital flows. We

have spent much time pointing this out for two reasons.
First, even though it will be suggested that the theory
of portfolio investment does not explain direct investment, the considerations just examined turn out to be
very important for the theory of direct investment.
For the imperfections of the capital market, which are
a difficulty for the theory of portfolio investment, are
precisely the factors which make the study of direct
investment interesting or, for that matter, relevant.

The second purpose is to justify one of the major
shortcomings of this presentation. A good theory of
direct investment should explain the differences in behavior between portfolio and direct investment. In
order to do this, there must be a theoretical explanation of portfolio investment. We have just tried to point
out the great difficulties in explaining the observed behavior of portfolio investment. It is, therefore, not
possible to treat here both direct and portfolio investment. Instead, we shall for the most part present an
explanation of direct investment and try to apply it
just to that form of investment.

Application of the Theory of Portfolio Investment to
Direct Investment

This, then, is the theory of portfolio investment. Does

it explain direct investment? We present here several features of direct investment which appear to be inconsistent with the interest-rate theory.

1. As the first illustration of one of the difficulties of using the theory of portfolio investment, the data in Table 1.3 on the national distribution of certain balance sheet items of a firm with investments in many countries should be considered.

There are three clear features. Total assets are distributed equally between the United States and the rest of the world. The liabilities of the firm are mostly in the rest of the world. Marketable securities and cash are mostly in the United States.

From the behavior of this firm, what can be inferred about interest rates? This table would indicate that interest rates are high in the United States and low in the rest of the world. The table appears to apply to a firm borrowing abroad and investing in the United States. Yet the table is the 1958 balance sheet of the Standard Oil Company of New Jersey, the largest single American direct investor. The figures in the balance sheet represent about 5 percent of the total United States direct investment.

Nor is the behavior of Standard Oil in any sense

Table 1.3 Area Distribution of Selected Balance Sheet Items of the Standard Oil Company (New Jersey), Fiscal Year 1958 (millions of dollars)

	United States	Amounts Located in Other Countries	All Countries
Total assets	4,880	4,598	9,478
Total liabilities	979	2,042	3,021
Net assets (total assets less total liabilities)	3,901	2,556	6,457
Cash and marketable securities (included in total assets above)	1,190	108	1,298
Net income	147	416	563
Net income as a percent of			
1. net assets	3.8%	16.3%	8.7%
2. total assets	3.0%	9.0%	5.9%
3. total assets excluding cash and marketable securities	4.0%	9.3%	6.9%

Source: 1958 Annual report of the Standard Oil Company (New Jersey).

atypical. The aggregate data on American investments
show the same features—those American firms which
invest abroad also borrow abroad. This is shown in
Table 1.4. It is quite evident that American-controlled
enterprises operating in foreign countries borrow substantial amounts abroad. In fact, the total American
investment of $11.8 billion is only slightly more than
half of the total assets of these enterprises. It is significant that most of the United States investments are
in equity capital, while most of the investments by
foreigners are in nonequity capital. (The table underestimates this feature, for as footnote a points out,
part of the foreign owners' investments are in bonds,
notes, and mortgages.) If this direct investment is
motivated by a desire to earn higher interest abroad,
this practice of borrowing substantially abroad seems
strange.

It is interesting to compare the balance sheet of the
Standard Oil Company of New Jersey with that of another large oil company with extensive worldwide
operations—the Royal Dutch Petroleum Company. Selected items from the 1958 annual report of this company are presented in Table 1.5. The behavior of Royal
Dutch is quite opposite to that of Standard Oil, for in

Table 1.4 Assets, Owners' Share, and Liabilities of U.S. Direct Investments, 1950 (billions of dollars)

	Total Assets	United States Investments		Foreign Owners' Invest-ment[a]	Liabilities to For-eigners[b]
		Equity Capital	Creditor Capital		
Total[c]	22.2	9.9	1.9	2.3	8.1
Areas					
Canada	6.8	3.0	.6	1.0	2.2
Latin American republics	7.4	3.9	.8	.3	2.4
Western Europe	4.4	1.5	.2	.4	2.3
Western European dependencies	.8	.3	.1	.2	.2
Other countries	2.8	1.1	.2	.4	1.1

[a] Includes equity in common stock and surplus, and bonds, notes, mortgages, and so forth.

[b] All other liabilities and reserves obtained by deducting the sum of columns 2, 3, and 4 from column 1.

[c] Totals may not add because of rounding.

Source: U.S. Department of Commerce, Office of Business Economics, Direct Private Foreign Investments of the United States Census of 1950 (Washington: U.S. Government Printing Office, 1953).

Table 1.5 Area Distribution of Selected Balance Sheet Items
of the Royal Dutch Petroleum Company, Fiscal Year 1958
(millions of pounds sterling)

	Europe and the Rest of the Eastern Hemisphere	Western Hemisphere United States	Other	Total
1. Long-term assets	660	347	490	1,497
2. Current assets less current liabilities	553	113	67	773
3. Long-term liabilities and minority interests	116	205	108	429
Net assets (item 1 plus item 2 less item 3)	1,097	255	449	1,801

Source: 1958 Annual report of the Royal Dutch Petroleum
Company.

relation to its total assets, Royal Dutch borrows heavily in the United States.

Here are two companies in the same industry, one
American and the other Dutch, and both of them invest and borrow in each other's countries and in other
parts of the world. It is hard to explain these investments simply in terms of interest rates, though it

could possibly be done; perhaps whatever paradoxes
there are might disappear if better information were
available. The point, however, is that in the theory of
direct investment that is proposed in this thesis, the
behavior we have just described is not at all strange
but in fact is exactly what one would expect.

2. The differences in behavior of direct and portfolio
investments just discussed in connection with the data
in Tables 1.1 and 1.2 hint that interest rates might
not account for the movements of both these types of
capital. The fact that they sometimes moved in opposite directions is particularly significant. The United
States began accumulating direct foreign investments
before 1914, at a time when it was still a large im-
porter of portfolio capital. In the postwar period there
have been flows of portfolio capital into the United
States, while the United States has been rapidly expanding its direct investments abroad. In fact, as can
be seen in Tables 1.1 and 1.6, in 1956 the United States
was a net debtor in portfolio investments.

The existence of cross movements may indicate that
the interest-rate theory cannot by itself explain the
movements of direct investment. The data on cross
movements were, in fact, introduced to support this

Table 1.6 United States Investments Abroad and Foreign Investments in the United States by Area, 1956 (billions of dollars)

	Direct Investments			Portfolio Investments		
	U.S. Investments Abroad	Foreign Investments in U.S.	Net U.S. Position	U.S. Investments Abroad	Foreign Investments in U.S.	Net U.S. Position
Europe[a]	3.5	2.9	.6	1.7	6.2	(4.5)[b]
Canada	7.5	1.5	6.0	4.3	1.2	3.1
Latin America	7.4	.1	7.3	.8	.8	0
Other	3.7	(-)[c]	3.7	1.2	.5	.7
Total[d]	22.1	4.5	17.6	7.9	8.8	(.9)[b]

[a] Europe is predominantly Western Europe.

[b] Figures in parentheses signify negative numbers.

[c] Less than $100,000,000.

[d] Totals may not add because of rounding.

Source: U.S. Department of Commerce, Office of Business Economics, Balance of Payments: Statistical Supplement, p. 181.

contention, but admittedly the cross movement could
be explained by the existence of risk and uncertainty
without contradicting the interest-rate theory, and this
possibility must be considered. Unfortunately, we know
of no way to test the hypothesis that risk and uncertainty account for these cross movements. We shall
try, however, in later chapters, to demonstrate that
there is another plausible reason.

3. Another feature which makes the interest-rate theory suspect as an explanation of direct investment is
the fact that most of the investment is made by firms
which operate preponderantly in the United States. For
these firms, foreign activities are only a small part of
total activities. This is shown in Table 1.7, which summarizes data on 442 companies with more than $1 mil-
lion of foreign investment in 1950 and accounting in
total for 85 percent of all United States direct foreign
investment. For the most part these firms are not
financial companies, and it is difficult to understand
why nonfinancial firms should be doing the foreign investing for the United States. It is more reasonable to
suppose that these investments have some motivation
other than the interest rate and that they are connected
with domestic activities of these firms. This is the

basis of the explanation we shall propose.

4. Direct investment has always shown a marked industrial distribution. It is possible for capital which moves in response to differences in interest rates to be associated with particular industries—although, in fact, portfolio capital was usually invested in government securities or very high grade bonds—but it would be unlikely that this association would take the form that it actually does. At any one point of time, portfolio capital would be invested in particular industries, but one would expect that as conditions changed, the capital invested in these industries would be withdrawn and invested in other industries and other countries. Yet the direct investments of the United States, at least, appear to be persistently associated with the same industries throughout this century. In the United Kingdom, for example, almost half of the labor force employed in United States-controlled enterprises in 1953 was employed in thirty-one firms which were established before 1914,[2] and as will to some extent be

[2] J. H. Dunning, American Investment in British Manufacturing Industry (London: George Allen and Unwin Ltd., 1958), p. 95.

Table 1.7 Total Assets and Foreign Assets of 442 Companies[a]
with Foreign Investments of One Million Dollars or More in
1950 (millions of dollars)

Industry[b]	Number of Companies	Total Assets 1949	Foreign Assets 1950	Foreign Assets as Percent of Total Assets
Extractive, total	64	20,367	4,705	23.1
Agriculture	12	747	544	72.8
Mining and smelting	26	6,639	881	13.3
Petroleum	26	12,981	3,280	25.3
Manufacturing, total	298	31,522	3,417	10.7
Food and kindred products	31	4,096	446	10.9
Paper and allied products	21	1,327	304	22.9
Chemical and allied products	39	5,122	387	7.6
Primary and fabricated metals	32	2,228	178	8.0
Machinery (except electrical)	50	3,718	546	14.7
Electrical equipment	19	2,960 ⎫		
Motor vehicles and equipment	19	6,222 ⎬	897	9.4
Other manufacturing	87	5,849	659	14.8
Service, trade, finance, insurance, miscellaneous, total	80	66,411	1,803	2.7
Public utilities	27	19,206	1,085	5.7
Trade	15	2,359	316	13.4
Miscellaneous	15	1,156	155	.6
Finance and insurance	23	43,690	247	1.3
Grand total	442	118,700	9,925	8.4

Table 1.7 Total Assets and Foreign Assets of 442 Companies[a] with Foreign Investments of One Million Dollars or More in 1950 (millions of dollars) (continued)

Industry[b]	Number of Companies	Total Assets 1949	Foreign Assets 1950	Foreign Assets as Percent of Total Assets
Total United States direct investment (1950 Census)		11,788		

[a]These 442 companies, each with foreign investments of $1 million or more, account for 85 percent of all direct foreign investment and 93 percent of all investments by U.S. companies.

[b]Industry classifications on the basis of the major activity abroad, considering all foreign operations of the parent company together.

Source: U.S. Department of Commerce, Office of Business Economics, Factors Limiting U.S. Investment Abroad: Part 2, Business Views on the U.S. Government's Role (Washington: U.S. Government Printing Office, 1954), pp. 52, 54.

shown in Chapter 4, many of the firms with large foreign investments began their foreign activities a good
while ago.

One would also expect that the industrial distribution
of investments motivated by the interest rate would be
quite different in one country than it is in another. Yet
direct investment appears to be associated with the
same industries throughout the world. If the investment is motivated by higher interest rates, it should
move to some countries and to all industries and not,
as is in fact the case, to some industries and to all
countries. It is almost true that wherever there was
or is oil, there was or is American direct investment,
and the same could be said for motor vehicles, business machinery, tires and tubes, soaps, farm machinery, and a long list of other commodities. Yet for
other industries, for example, cotton textiles, clothing, leather, printing, and primary iron and steel,
the United States has almost no direct investment.

Furthermore, and this is very important, cross investment often occurs within industries. With one exception, in each of the industries listed earlier, one
of the large firms which operate in the United States
is a foreign firm: Shell Oil, Dunlop Tire and Rubber,

Moore Business Forms, and now Olivetti, Lever
Brothers, and Massey-Harris-Ferguson. The one exception is automobiles. It is not certain that this will
remain an exception very long.

This is all the evidence to be offered now on the difficulties of using interest rates to explain direct investment. Instead, we turn to proposing a different
explanation.

The Theory of Direct Investment

Why, then, direct investment? The important theoretical shortcoming of the interest-rate theory is that it
does not explain control. If interest rates are higher
abroad than at home, an investor will do well to lend
money abroad, but there is no logical necessity for
him to control the enterprise he lends to. If we wish
to explain direct investment, we must explain control.

There are two main types of reasons why an investor
will seek control. The first, which I shall call direct
investment, Type 1, has to do with the prudent use of
assets. The investor seeks control over the enterprise in order to ensure the safety of his investment.
This reason applies to domestic investment as well.
If the entrepreneur has no funds of his own in the enterprise he controls, his incentive not to go into bank-

ruptcy is lessened. This is especially important in international investment where there is an inherent conflict of interest between investors of different nationality over how much reserves are to be kept in a particular currency. There also appears to be considerably more distrust in international transactions than in intranational and therefore more incentive for the capitalist to seek control. Whether the view that foreigners are less trustworthy than natives is in fact justified is irrelevant. All that is necessary is that investors feel that way, or that borrowers and governments feel differently about external defaults than they do about internal defaults.

The theory of Type 1 direct investment is very similar to the theory of portfolio investment. The interest rate is the key factor in both. Direct investment of Type 1 will substitute for portfolio investment when the distrust of foreigners is high or when fear of expropriation and risks of exchange-rate changes are high, but its movements will still be in response to differences in the interest rate. The same objections just given to the theory of portfolio investment as an explanation of the direct investment observed also apply to the theory of direct investment of Type 1.

There is another type of direct investment that does
not depend on the interest rate and which I shall call
direct investment of Type 2, or international operations. In this second type of direct investment, the
motivation for controlling the foreign enterprise is not
the prudent use of assets but something quite different.
The control of the foreign enterprise is desired in order to remove competition between that foreign enterprise and enterprises in other countries. Or the control is desired in order to appropriate fully the returns
on certain skills and abilities.

It frequently happens that enterprises in different
countries compete with each other because they sell in
the same market or because some of the firms sell to
other firms. If the markets are imperfect, that is, if
there is horizontal or bilateral monopoly or oligopoly,
some form of collusion will be profitable. One form
of collusion is to have the various enterprises owned
and controlled by one firm. This is one motivation
for firms to control enterprises in foreign countries.

The other main motivation stems from the fact that
firms are very unequal in their ability to operate in a
particular industry. A firm with advantages over other
firms in the production of a particular product may

find it profitable to undertake the production of this product in a foreign country as well. The firm could also rent or sell its skill rather than undertake itself the foreign production. Which method it chooses depends largely on the degree of imperfection in the market for the skill. If the market is imperfect, the owner may not be able to appropriate fully the returns to the ability unless he controls its use.

These, then, are the two main reasons why nationals of one country find it profitable to control enterprises in another country apart from the desire to ensure the prudent use of assets. Much direct investment which occurs may well be the capital movements associated with the financing of these international operations of firms. The demand for American direct investment is then the demand by Americans for capital to finance their own foreign activities; this is in contrast to the demand for capital by entrepreneurs of other countries for their activities.

In part, the capital movement is needed to acquire a share of the foreign enterprise and thus obtain the desired control. The motivation for the investment is not the higher interest rate abroad but the profits that are derived from controlling the foreign enterprise.

Aside from the minimum investment needed to acquire
a controlling interest, other international capital
movements might occur in connection with the financing of the international operation. The task of Chapter
5 is to explore this question of the amount of capital
movement associated with international operations.
The importance and interest of this subject turn out
to depend entirely on the imperfections in the capital
market. If capital markets were perfect, so that interest rates were identical everywhere, then firms
would be quite indifferent as to where they obtained
finance, and where they financed would make no difference in the determination of interest rates or the
supply of capital in each country. When imperfections
are introduced, the answer to the question of how capital is associated with direct investment is not a simple
one, and, as was implied earlier in the comparison
between Royal Dutch and Standard Oil (New Jersey), it
is not independent of the nationality of the firm.

The International Operations of National Firms

The theory of international operations is part of the
theory of the firm. It is concerned with the various
relationships between enterprises of one country and
enterprises of another. More particularly, it is con-

cerned with the conditions under which an enterprise
of one country will be controlled by a firm of another
country or enterprises in several countries will be
controlled by the same firm. It is a problem of determining the extent of vertical and horizontal integration
of firms. The tools used to analyze international operations are the same, essentially, as those used to analyze the firm in its operations. But there are two important differences: the operations are international,
and the firms are national.

Because the operations are international, many
things must be taken into consideration which would
not be important in interregional economics. Different
nations have different governments, different laws,
different languages, and different economies; and communications between countries has, in the past at least,
typically been far less than between regions within a
country. Because of this, the markets of different
countries are much more separate than the markets
of different regions. This lack of integration can be
quite important. It provides a good deal of the interest in the subject of international operations, especially since it may be fast disappearing. In recent years,
there has been a great increase in communications be-

tween nations, and we may be watching the integration
of the world economy or at least the economic integration of broader areas than in the past. The increased
international operations may be a result of this, and
they may also play their part in furthering integration,
just as the emergence of the national firm allegedly
did in countries like the United States. We shall see.
But it has not happened yet, and the firms are national
firms and not international firms. Their nationality is
of the utmost importance, for it affects the way they
behave, and it affects the treatment they receive.

There are at least three senses in which a firm has
a nationality. First it has a legal nationality, and this
determines the legal limitations on its behavior. A
firm also has nationality because most of its shareholders reside in a certain nation, and, what is more
important, it is committed to pay dividends in a certain currency. Last and probably least, the managers
of the firm have a nationality, and this may affect their
allegiance and the firm's behavior.

The difference in treatment because of nationality is
well known. Nearly all countries now have restrictions,
sometimes very severe, on the activity of foreign concerns. And the problem of expropriation is ever present.

The behavior of a firm depends on its nationality partly because it is subject to control and taxation by its own government and partly because it may have nationalist sentiments. But most important is the fact that it is interested in eventually receiving its profits in its own currency. This is why there is a transfer problem. A firm will always attach a risk premium to any investment in a foreign country that it does not attach to its domestic investments. If the costs are similar, the firm will prefer, for example, to build a research center at home rather than abroad. It will also be concerned about keeping reserves in its own currency.

Conclusion

We have tried to suggest in this chapter that the interest-rate theory does not explain the movement of direct investment from country to country. Instead, we proposed that direct investments are the capital movements associated with the international operations of firms. To understand direct investment, both international operations and their financing must therefore be studied. The study of international operations will occupy three chapters; one to state the theory, one to derive its implications, and one to examine such empirical evidence on the subject as exists. The study of the financing of international operations will take one chapter. The final chapter will deal with some of the effects of international operations and the very limited implications of these effects for policy.

2

THE THEORY OF INTERNATIONAL OPERATIONS—PART I

Introduction

Some enterprises in a particular country are entirely controlled by nationals of that country; other enterprises are entirely controlled by foreigners. In between these two extremes there is a wide variety of relationships. The enterprise may be a joint venture, half-owned by nationals and half-owned by foreigners; or the partnership may be unequal: either nationals or foreigners may have only a minority interest. The foreigner may have no ownership at all yet still exercise some control through a licensing agreement or a cartel. The relationship may be more subtle; tacit collusion among the enterprises is possible. The relationship then is still very real, though it does not take an overt form. The various types of relationships between business enterprises in one country and enterprises in another country make up the subject matter of international operations.

There are two dimensions to the relationship. One is the amount of control one enterprise has over another, that is, the extent to which decisions of one enterprise are affected directly by the other enterprises; the other is the legal ownership, that is, the percent of the equity of a corporation owned by another corporation. The two dimensions are connected, though not precisely, for ownership of equity securities is one way of achieving control. If this method is used, direct investment occurs; and as was suggested in Chapter 1, a substantial part of United States direct investment may very well be of this type. The financial aspects of the subject will be explored in more detail later. In this chapter we are interested in examining the control relationships.

We want to know the circumstances that cause a firm to control an enterprise in a foreign country. Two major reasons and one minor one can be distinguished. The two major reasons are as follows:

1. It is sometimes profitable to control enterprises in more than one country in order to remove competition between them.

2. Some firms have advantages in a particular activity, and they may find it profitable to exploit these advantages by establishing foreign operations.

The minor reason, which for convenience is discussed in between the discussion of the major reasons, is diversification. It is minor because control is not necessarily involved. But before those reasons are discussed, we shall discuss some of the barriers to international operations.

Barriers to International Operations—the Advantages of National Firms in Their Home Market

In the absence of special features, the enterprises operating in a country are likely to be national firms, for national firms are likely to have advantages over foreigners. This is precisely because we are dealing with international rather than interregional economics. Though it is not always true, national economics are usually more isolated from each other than interregional economics, and communication between them is more costly. National firms have the general advantage of better information about their country: its economy, its language, its law, and its politics. To a foreigner the cost of acquiring this information may be considerable. But note that it is a fixed cost; once incurred by establishing a foreign operation, it need not be incurred again.

Of a more permanent nature is the barrier to international operations arising from discrimination by government, by consumers, and by suppliers. It is not the general treatment that is important: this affects the domestic firms as well as the foreign firms, but it does not give one firm an advantage over another. What is important is the fact that in given countries,

foreigners and nationals may receive very different
treatment. The government discrimination can be extreme. There may be outright prohibition of foreigners
or severe restrictions on the types of activity foreigners are permitted to engage in. And the danger of expropriation is usually greater for foreigners than for
natives. It is hard to tell whether consumers or suppliers really care about the nationality of the firm they
deal with. Sometimes it is found to be important, but
little is known about this aspect of the stigma of being
foreign. Foreigners may also have disadvantages—or
for that matter, advantages—because of their own
government's actions, for the international operations
are affected by the laws of the home country. Ford of
Canada was prohibited by the United States State Department from selling automobiles to China even though
it would have been legal for a Canadian company to do
so. Income from foreign operations is subject to taxation by the government of the parent concern.

Of great importance as a barrier is the exchange-
rate risk. A change in the exchange rate affects nationals and foreigners quite differently. If the franc
depreciates, all holders of francs lose. But those
planning to spend francs in France lose less than those

planning to spend the value of the money in the United
States; for there are some goods which are not inter-
nationally traded, the price of which in francs may not
change at all or at least not by as much as the price
of other goods. A company which must pay its dividends
in dollars must take this into consideration when deciding to invest in France. If a firm were truly international, so that its liabilities each year in any currency were proportionate to its income in that currency,
it would be no more concerned about changes in the exchange rate than American firms are concerned about
devaluations of the dollar when they decide to invest in
America.

There is great difficulty in studying these advantages
of national firms in their home market, for they are
extremely difficult to measure. This is unfortunate
since they can be extremely important. It would be
very interesting in any case to find out, but information on the subject is sorely lacking. So we must stop
here and turn to the reason why firms, despite the disadvantages, still find it profitable to have foreign operations.

Removal of Conflict as a Cause of International Operations

Enterprises in different countries frequently are connected to each other through markets. They compete
by selling in the same market, or one of the firms
may sell to the other. If such a connection exists, it
may be profitable to have one firm controlling all the
enterprises rather than having separate firms in each
country. In other words, it is profitable to substitute
centralized decision making for decentralized decision
making. Whether or not this will occur depends mainly
on whether the markets are perfect.

Take first an extreme case of horizontal competition.
Suppose there are two countries, and in each country
only one firm, because of great economies of scale in
production. If international trade is possible, the situation is one of duopoly, and some form of collusion is
profitable. One form of collusion is merger. If a
merger occurs, competition between the two units is
eliminated, and total profits are increased. If we have
more than two countries and more than one firm in
each country, then the case is more complicated, but
the principle is the same as long as two conditions are
present: first, that there is competition, potential or

actual, between the enterprises of the different countries; second, entry is difficult, and there are only a
few firms. If entry is not difficult, there is not much
point in trying to control the market. Whatever increase in profits might be achieved will soon be lost
because of the entry of new firms. When there are
more than a few firms, cooperation becomes more difficult.

To an empirical researcher this case is difficult to
handle. Suppose he finds an industry where the two
conditions prevail. Then merger is possible, but not
necessary. Other forms of collusion are possible. Or
the firms may not collude and not achieve joint maximization. Unfortunately, there is not much theory to
guide him as to which result is more likely.

Similar considerations apply when firms of one country sell to firms of another country and where there
are only a few buyers and a few sellers. In this case
a bilateral monopoly situation occurs. Again merger
is one form of cooperation to increase joint profit,
and again it is not a necessary result.

This is probably an important reason for international operations where raw materials are involved.
In many cases where international operations occur—

copper, iron ore, bauxite, aluminum, and oil—there
are only a few buyers of the raw materials and, because of technological considerations, only a few producers. Certainly the great concern about transfer
prices in taxation questions hints that sequential monopoly is involved.

In both the horizontal and vertical cases we have
outlined situations where it may be profitable to have
one firm. But what will be the nationality of the firm?
There is nothing inherent in the theory to determine
this. Other considerations may dominate, such as the
particular entrepreneurs involved or the historical
sequence. Suppose a new copper mine is discovered
whose value is small compared to the size of the ex-
isting copper companies. One would then expect that
it would be easier for the copper companies to buy control of the new mine than for the mine owners to buy
control of the copper companies.

Before discussing the other major cause of international operations—that is, the possession of advantages—it is convenient to discuss diversification as a
cause of something that is not quite international operations but is associated with it.

Diversification as a Motivation for International Operations

It sometimes happens that profits in one line of activity are inversely correlated with profits in another line of activity. For example, aluminum plants need large quantities of electricity. If a plant is built in an under-developed area where electricity is cheap, the possibility exists that the area will in the future become developed. In that case, the price of electricity will rise, profits to the aluminum producer will decline, and rents to the electric power plants will rise. Many examples of this type of correlation are possible, especially in the case of raw materials. When they occur, there is a good opportunity for diversification. The fact of high negative correlation means that an investor who invests both in aluminum plants and in their power supply greatly reduces the risk of his investment. This may be one reason why firms will engage in both activities. But it is important to stress that the firm need not control the enterprise; in fact, the firm need not have anything at all to do with it. The shareholders of the firm can, if they wish, stabilize their profits by buying shares of two different companies, each engaging in only one of the activities. The

main reason why the firm may do it rather than leave
it to shareholders may be that it has more information.

This reason for international operations does not involve control and is not really the same as the other
reasons. But indubitably it plays its part, and most
likely it is closely associated with the removal of the
competition argument just discussed.

The Possession of Advantages as a Cause of International Operations

Firms are by no means equal in their ability to operate
in an industry. Certain firms have considerable advantages in particular activities. The possession of these
advantages may cause them to have extensive international operations of one kind or another. The firm will
in some cases license its advantages to a local firm;
in other cases it will itself operate the foreign enterprise.

There are as many kinds of advantages as there are
functions in making and selling a product. The firm's
advantage may be that it can acquire factors of production at a lower cost than other firms. Or it may have
knowledge or control of a more efficient production
function. Or the firm may have better distribution

facilities or a differentiated product.

Bain has carefully analyzed the types and strength of advantages in connection with his study of the conditions of entry.[1] His analysis is extremely relevant here, with appropriate adjustments for the fact that it is used in a different context. Bain is interested in the advantages which established firms have relative to new firms insofar as these advantages determine profits. We are interested in the advantages possessed by firms of one country relative to firms of another country insofar as these determine the nationality of the firm conducting a certain enterprise. That is, we are interested in the barriers to entry, not as they apply to new firms, but as they apply to firms of a different

[1] J. S. Bain, Barriers to New Competition (Cambridge, Mass.: Harvard University Press, 1956). Table 2.1 reproduces his summary table of the advantages possessed by firms and the circumstances in which they arise. His book contains empirical estimates of the strength of these advantages for twenty industries. Unfortunately, in the field of international operations, the kinds of advantages and circumstances that are relevant and important are not known, and it would be an extremely fruitful area of research to do for international operations what Bain has done for national. We do not do so here for many reasons, and the strength and importance of our hypotheses suffer accordingly.

nationality.

The advantages that a firm possesses relative to a firm of its own country may be quite different from the advantages it possesses relative to firms of another country. A firm may have advantages in a certain industry, but international operations are concerned with a certain industry in a particular country. In the foreign country, the firm is subject to all the disadvantages (or advantages) of being foreign that were discussed previously. For this reason the strength of the advantages of particular firms are usually less abroad than at home.

But for other reasons a firm's advantages may be more potent abroad than at home. In the United States a firm is subject to competition from a large number of entrepreneurs who possess equal access to general factors of production such as skilled personnel and capital. But in the foreign countries there may be an extreme shortage of entrepreneurs and skilled personnel, and the capital market may be very poor. Moreover—and this is critical—the foreigner may not have access to the general fund of ability and capital in the United States because of the lack of integration in the world economy.

Table 2.1 Summary Table of Bain's Description of Advantages of Established Firms and the Circumstances in Which They Arise

---

I. Typical circumstances giving rise to an absolute cost advantage to established firms

    A. Control of production techniques by established firms, via either patents or secrecy. (Such control may permit exclusion of entrants from access to optimal techniques, or alternatively the levying of a discriminatory royalty charge for their use.)

    B. Imperfections in the markets for hired factors of production (e.g., labor, materials, etc.) which allow lower buying prices to established firms; alternatively ownership or control of strategic factor supplies (e.g., resources) by established firms, which permits either exclusion of entrants from such supplies, driving entrants to use inferior supplies, or discriminatory pricing of supplies to them.

    C. Significant limitations of the supplies of productive factors in specific markets or submarkets for them, relative to the demands of an efficient entrant firm. Then an increment to entry will perceptibly increase factor prices.

    D. Money-market conditions imposing higher interest rates upon potential entrants than upon established firms. (These conditions are apparently more likely to be effective as a source of advantage to established firms as the absolute capital requirement for an efficient entrant increases.)

II. Typical circumstances giving rise to a product differentiation advantage to established firms

    A. The accumulative preference of buyers for established brand names and company reputations, either generally or except for small minorities of buyers.

    B. Control of superior product designs by established firms through patents, permitting either exclusion of entrants from them or the levying of discriminatory royalty charges.

Table 2.1 Summary Table of Bain's Description of Advantages of Established Firms and the Circumstances in Which They Arise (continued)

    C. Ownership or contractual control by established firms of favored distributive outlets, in situations where the supply of further outlets is other than perfectly elastic.

III. Typical circumstances discouraging entry by sustaining significant economies of the large-scale firm

    A. Real economies (i.e., in terms of quantities of factors used per unit of output) of large-scale production and distribution such that an optimal firm will supply a significant share of the market.

    B. Strictly pecuniary economies (i.e., monetary economies only, such as those due to the greater bargaining power of large buyers) of large-scale production, having a similar effect.

    C. Real or strictly pecuniary economies of large-scale advertising or other sales promotion, having a similar effect.

Source: Quoted verbatim from J. S. Bain, Barriers to New Competition, (Cambridge, Mass.: Harvard University Press, 1956), pp. 15-16.

A skilled American might very well be willing to
work abroad for an American firm, while he would be
quite unwilling to do so for a foreign firm. His preference might stem from his desire to ensure himself of
a position in the United States should he in later years
wish to return home. Other considerations of political
and national allegiance might also arise.

Something similar to this may be true of the capital
market. It is sometimes felt that the New York capital
market, through inertia, ignorance, or irrationality,
discriminates among borrowers of equal worth accord-
ing to their nationality, even after the appropriate dis-
counts for real special costs are made.

Because a firm possesses advantages, its business
enterprise in the foreign country would be profitable.
Because international operations are motivated by
these profits, there can be direct investment even
when there is not enough of an interest-rate difference
to cause portfolio investment. Unequal ability of firms
is a sufficient condition for international operations.
The rest of this chapter is concerned with the fact that
it is not a necessary condition.

The Possibility of Licensing

If a firm of one country possesses an advantage over

firms of all other countries in a certain line of activity, that does not necessarily mean that the firm will have its own enterprises in foreign countries. For one thing, the firm could export the commodity in which the advantage is embodied. These cases are easily identifiable, for the product is not produced abroad. A more interesting reason why the firm will not itself have a foreign operation is that the firm can often license, rent, or otherwise sell its advantage.

This is frequently the case. We find some firms with no foreign enterprises but extensive licensing arrangements. Other firms have subsidiaries in some countries and licenses in other countries. Occasionally, the firm has operations abroad and licenses at home.

To study the role advantages play in explaining international operations, we must examine some of the aspects which go into a firm's decision to license. We do not attempt a complete analysis. We only point out certain aspects which will be relevant in future discussion. It is important to do this because whether the firm sells the skills or whether the firm sells the product containing the skills determines to a large extent the amount of direct investment it makes.

Why does a firm use the advantage itself instead of

licensing it? We can view the problem this way. The firm is a practical institutional device which substitutes for the market. The firm internalizes or supersedes the market. A fruitful approach to our problem is to ask why the market is an inferior method of exploiting the advantage; that is, we look at imperfections in the market.

One line of thought immediately presents itself. Decentralized decision making—a free market—is defective when there are certain types of interactions between the firms; that is, each firm's behavior noticeably affects the other firms'. If each firm pursues its own interest, joint maximization may very well not occur. In this case the problem can be alleviated by central control and ownership. Under common ownership an attempt is made to maximize joint rather than individual profits. In other words, the same considerations of horizontal oligopoly and bilateral monopoly as discussed earlier apply here.

Consider a firm deciding whether to license its advantage in a particular industry. Suppose that in this particular industry technical considerations are such that there will be only one or, at most, a few firms in each market. If the firm attempts to license its prod-

ucts, it will encounter two problems which could be
solved by owning the operating enterprises. In the
first place, it will be selling its advantage to enterprises which possess monopoly power in their markets.
A sequential monopoly problem is therefore involved.
Integration could then increase joint profits. The second problem of licensing arises from the difficulty of
controlling price and output. To achieve maximum
profits, a firm which licenses must specify the precise
use to each firm, and this is not always possible under
the antitrust laws. Alternatively, it could let the firms
compete, but this may result in a loss of profits. If
the firm which possesses the advantages does not
license but instead undertakes the operations itself,
there is less difficulty in achieving maximum profits.
It is important to stress that both of these reasons for
not licensing disappear if there are many buyers of
the advantage. It is the market impurity which leads
the possessor of the advantage to choose to supersede
the market for his advantage. It should also be noted
that the sequential monopoly problem does not require
complete control over the licenses. A minority interest will often suffice. If there is a minority interest
and no direct charge for the license, the distortion

problem of sequential monopoly no longer arises.

Impurities in the market are not the only kind of
imperfections which are relevant here. In a world of
uncertainty there may be a conflict of evaluations,
which make cooperation difficult. Business is risky,
and businessmen receive signals but not complete information. People read signals differently and so act
differently even where their goals are identical. Hence
there is a difficulty of reaching an agreement between
the licenser and the licensee. The owner of the advantage may use it himself because his evaluation of
it is different from the evaluation of other people because he has more information about his advantage
and a greater incentive to use it.

Aside from causing a conflict of evaluations, uncertainty makes it difficult for buyers and sellers to
achieve a satisfactory licensing contract. If the contract contains rigid provisions, changing conditions
will hurt one party and benefit the other. A more flex-
ible type of arrangement may be advantageous—a
partnership with sharing of profits, for example.

A reluctance to license may also arise from the inherent danger of losing the advantage. The licensee
may discover a process which substitutes for the ad-

vantage. Or he may develop consumer ties or other affiliations which give him advantages. In this case a profit-sharing arrangement will protect the possessor of the advantage.

Most of these considerations imply that it is preferable for the firm to operate itself rather than to license. But on the other side is the very important fact that there do exist other firms in other countries with advantages of their own. It may not pay to compete with these other firms, and so some form of cooperation such as licensing may arise. If there are many other firms, licensing is almost certain. But a problem arises when there are only a few firms. Here cooperation through licensing is difficult because a bilateral monopoly problem is involved. The firm may then establish foreign operations.

The considerations just outlined apply equally well to domestic as to foreign exploitation of an advantage. We should, therefore, expect great similarity in the national structure of firms and the international. However, there are differences; firms often license abroad in areas where they operate at home. The difference, of course, is due to the difference between interregional and international trade.

A firm deciding on the best method of exploiting its
advantage in a country other than its own may find itself at a considerable disadvantage if it wants to establish a foreign subsidiary. In the most extreme case
it might be prohibited by government from operating
in that country. It then has no choice but to license if
it is to get any revenue at all. Most likely its disadvantage will be less extreme. But there will be some
merit in cooperating with local firms, in some form
or other, if the local firms have some advantages of
operating in that country. In particular, the exchange-
rate risk is nearly always present if the firm undertakes the operation itself. To reduce its risk, it can
recruit local capital, and the only way to do this may
be to allow local participation. It is interesting that the
extent of local participation in United States foreign enterprises is slightly greater for those started after the
war than for those started before the war.[2] But there
is not enough information to tell whether this is actually due to the increased nationalism which some ob-

[2]U.S. Department of Commerce, Office of Business
Economics, Direct Private Foreign Investments of the
United States: Census of 1950 (Washington: U.S. Gov-
ernment Printing Office, 1953), p. 23.

servers feel has characterized recent years.

There is another reason why a firm looking abroad is likely to find firms with which it is better to cooperate than compete. For many reasons international markets have been more separate from each other than markets within a country. Communication in the past was poor, and transport costs were high. In this milieu independent local firms might arise sheltered, as it were, from the competition of foreigners. When communications improve, or when firms become sufficiently large to surmount the problems of long-distance coordination, the local firms may very well be established. Since there already is a local firm, the firm has a choice of licensing, merging, or establishing a subsidiary. Exactly what it does is not easily predicted. The answer depends on some of the considerations outlined above, and even then the outcome is not certain—the indeterminacy of oligopoly situations recurs.

Within a country there is more integration, and it is more likely that the profit-maximizing position has been reached. In international affairs, where international economies have in the past been poorly integrated, we are more likely to be observing a transitory relation-

ship in which licensing will be one characteristic. It
is interesting that some companies begin by licensing,
then acquire minority interest, and ultimately acquire
control. The sequence can also work in the opposite
direction. The firm may be operating abroad where it
would license at home because there are no local firms
to license to. This is especially likely in underdeveloped countries. Through time, in these countries,
local firms may develop, the foreign operations decline, and licensing be substituted.

Another reason for the greater predominance of licensing abroad than at home is the increased possibility of dividing markets in the international economy.
The reason may be that tariffs and transport costs
separate markets or that antitrust laws are more
loosely applied. In this case the firm can discriminate
between markets through licensing arrangements without itself establishing foreign operations.

Some Empirical Evidence on International Licensing
Arrangements of United States Firms

There is some empirical evidence on the extent to
which firms resort to licensing in their foreign activities. It is neither very good nor very plentiful, but
it does illustrate what we have been talking about. The

data are presented in Tables 2.2 and 2.3, which show
the national and industrial distribution of the receipts
and payments of United States firms in connection with
licensing—or more correctly, in connection with all
agreements to supply patents, processes, technology,
equipment under rental, and other technical and proprietary assets such as copyrights and trademarks.

Total receipts of United States companies from rents,
royalties, and the like from unaffiliated foreign companies were $128.4 million in 1956. This amount is
large compared to payments by United States firms of
$22.5 million but small compared to the $3.134 billion
of earnings on all direct investments. However, it is
significant compared to the $858 million of earnings
on direct investments in manufacturing (which is probably the more appropriate figure for comparison since
most licensing occurs in the manufacturing sector),
and it is especially significant in the case of certain
countries.

Canada and Latin America present a similar pattern.
The receipts from unaffiliated companies are completely
overshadowed by earnings on manufacturing investments
and receipts from affiliated companies. (The affiliated
companies are branch plants and subsidiaries which

Table 2.2 License[a] Receipts and Payments of United States
Firms, and Earnings on Direct Investments by Area and
Country in 1956 (millions of dollars)

| (1) | License[a] Receipts of U.S. Companies from Foreigners | |
	Unaffiliated Companies	Affiliates[b] of U.S. Companies
(1)	(2)	(3)
Canada	15.7	49.6
Latin America	10.4	75.0
Brazil	2.7	11.5
Mexico	2.7	8.3
Other	5.0	55.2
Continental Europe	50.3	36.4
France	18.6	11.5
Germany	11.8	13.8
Italy	9.4	3.4
Netherlands	3.0	1.1
Belgium	2.2	2.0
Switzerland	.4	.9
Sweden	2.1	1.2
Other	2.8	2.5
Sterling area	36.7	42.5
United Kingdom	28.6	22.3
Australia	5.1	7.2 ⎫
Other	3.0	13.0 ⎭

License[a] Payments by U.S. Companies to Foreigners	Earnings on U.S. Direct Investment	
	Manufacturing	All Industries
(4)	(5)	(6)
.9	393	701
.3	125	1,052
N.A.	38	79
N.A.	37	80
N.A.	50	893
12.2	107	201
6.1	36	51
2.3	33	53
.7	9	22
.6	3	19
.5	11	19
1.1	7	11
.3	5	8
.6	3	18
9.0	N.A.	N.A.
8.9	139	273
	41	67
.1	N.A.	N.A.

Table 2.2 License[a] Receipts and Payments of United States
Firms, and Earnings on Direct Investments by Area and
Country in 1956 (millions of dollars) (continued)

	License[a] Receipts of U.S. Companies from Foreigners	
	Unaffiliated Companies	Affiliates[b] of U.S. Companies
Other countries	15.3	25.0
Japan	11.8	3.8
Other	3.5	21.2
Total	128.4	228.5

N.A. Not available.

[a]Receipts and payments refer not only to licensing but to all
receipts and payments in connection with agreements to supply
patents, processes, technology, equipment under rental, and
other technical and proprietary assets such as copyrights and
trademarks.

[b]Affiliates of United States companies refer to foreign branches
and subsidiaries. The receipts from affiliates do not include
receipts paid by foreigners to these foreign branches and subsidiaries but remitted in the form of profits or dividends to
the parent firm.

Sources: Columns 1, 2, 3, 4. J. B. Smith, "U.S. Firms Con-
duct Lively Technical Exchanges with Foreign Companies,"
Foreign Commerce Weekly, December 29, 1958, pp. 1-3.
Columns 5 and 6. S. Pizer and F. Cutler, "Growth of Foreign
Investments in the United States and Abroad," Survey of Cur-
rent Business, XXXVII (August 1957), p. 25.

License[a] Payments by U.S. Companies to Foreigners	Earnings on U.S. Direct Investment	
	Manufacturing	All Industries
.1		
N. A.	10	23
N. A.		
22.5	858	3,134

Table 2.3 License[a] Receipts and Payments of United States
Firms by Industry in 1956 (millions of dollars)

	Receipts of U.S. Companies from Foreigners	Payments by U.S. Companies to Foreigners
Food, including tobacco	1.2	.2
Textiles and allied	5.7	.5
Chemical and allied	25.2	10.5
Rubber products	1.6	N.A.
Primary and fabricated metals	8.1	1.6
Machinery (except electrical)	23.2	1.3
Electrical machinery	21.0	.7
Motor vehicles and equipment	5.6	.5
Other transportation	11.0	1.8
Petroleum	8.9	.2
All other	16.9	5.2
Total, all industries	128.4	22.5

[a]Receipts and payments refer not only to licensing but to all
receipts and payments in connection with agreements to supply patents, processes, technology, equipment under rental,
and other technical and proprietary assets such as copyright
and trademarks.
Source: Smith, "U.S. Firms Conduct Lively Technical Exchanges with Foreign Companies," p. 2.

probably are classified as direct investments, and the receipts from these may be included in earnings on direct investment.) There are almost no payments by United States firms to firms in Canada and Latin America. As will be discussed in the next two chapters, the ratio of direct investment to national income is much higher for these countries than for the rest of the world, and the share of their industries controlled by foreigners is higher. All these facts point in the same direction: there are relatively fewer native firms in Canada and Latin America able to compete with American firms, as compared to Europe. For in Europe, all these relationships reverse themselves. Receipts from unaffiliated companies are high, as compared to affiliated companies and as compared to earnings on manufacturing direct investments. Payments to Europeans are also higher. And the share of America in European industry is, in general, less than in Canadian or Latin American industry. These facts all point to the existence of stronger local competition for American industry in Europe.

The pattern of licensing and direct investment in the rest of the world is very similar to that of Canada and the Latin American countries and dissimilar to Europe.

This is what one would expect. There are two exceptions: Japan, which is similar to Europe in all respects, and Australia, where the receipts from unaffiliated firms are relatively high. For Australia, no
explanation is offered. For Japan, the heavy reliance
on licensing may be due to government control.

One interesting point about the industrial distribution shown in Table 2.3 may be noted. In the chemical
industry, both receipts and payments are high. This
suggests that both Americans and Europeans (notably
French and German) have advantages in this industry—
suggestion which is further supported by the fact that
there used to be considerable foreign direct investment in the United States in chemicals, and if it had
not been for the war, there might still be. In this context it is interesting to compare the national distribution of direct investment in chemicals to the distribution of investment for all manufacturing industries.
This is done in Table 2.4 for 1955, the latest year for
which this type of information is available. The investment in Europe is, relative to investment in all
countries, proportionally less for chemicals than for
all manufacturing. It is also known that European
chemical firms have direct investments in other

Table 2.4   United States Direct Investment in All Manufacturing and in Chemicals and Allied Products, Area Distribution,
1955 (millions of dollars)

	Investment in All Manufacturing[a]	Investment in Chemicals and Allied Products
Canada	2,834	311
Latin America	1,366	407
Europe	1,631	157
Other areas	491	70
Total	6,322	945

[a]Includes manufacturing operation of petroleum and mining
companies.
Source: Pizer and Cutler, "Growth of Foreign Investments in
the United States and Abroad," p. 22.

countries.[3] This may reflect market sharing of some
kind.

This concludes the initial statement of the theory of
international operations. In the next chapter some implications of the theory will be discussed.

[3] For example, European direct investment in the
chemical industry in Brazil is as great as American
investment there. See Stanford Research Institute,
International Industrial Development Centre, International Comparative Studies, Investment Series 1,
Brazil—Factors Affecting Foreign Investment (Menlo
Park, Calif. : Stanford Research Institute, 1958),
p. 29.

3
THE THEORY OF INTERNATIONAL OPERATIONS—
PART II

In the last chapter we presented the theory of interna-

tional operations. We specified two major and one

minor cause, and we related these causes to the form

of international operations. In this chapter we try to

bring the various points together in a systematic fashion

that illustrates their implications. The material of this

chapter is largely repetitious.

The Many Forms of International Operations

The basis of the theory of international operations is

the connection between enterprises in various coun-

tries. There are many kinds of interrelations, and the

form of an international operation depends in part on

which kind prevails. The various relations center on

horizontal or vertical competition between the units or

on the possession by nationals of one country of an ad-

vantage which they exploit in another country. The

forms we observe are branch plant, wholly owned sub-

sidiary, majority-owned subsidiary, joint venture,

minority interest, licensing arrangement, and tacit

collusion.[1]

[1] For an extensive description of the many forms—
agent, representatives, branch house, fully controlled
subsidiary, minority interest, concession, contract,

There is no simple connection between the overt form
and the underlying relation, for there are many ways to
achieve the same goal. We cannot be sure that a firm
with 50 percent of the stock of a company exercises
more control than a firm with 25 percent or a licensing
arrangement. It would take a very detailed study of
firms to specify the nature and extent of the influence.
It would, I think, be a very interesting study. Much is
made of control by changing forms. In these discus-
sions there often is no explicit consideration of the
many kinds of control and the many forms which can
be used to achieve any one of them.

Don Cotton[2] has suggested an interesting hypothesis
which illustrates the difference between changing the
form and changing the fundamental relationship. He
suggests that a company forced by governments to allow greater local participation in its foreign subsidiary
will overcome this change in form by enforcing more
centralized decision making. Nationals of the country

---

and licensing agreement—used by American firms op-
erating in Europe in 1931, see F. A. Southard, Jr.,
American Industry in Europe (Boston: Houghton Mifflin
Company, 1931), Chapter 1.

[2] In the draft of a thesis being prepared at M.I.T.

of the subsidiary will be participating, but the decision will be made in the head office.

The forms depend in part on the type of control desired. If the motivation is to separate markets and prevent competition between units, then the control of price and output decisions must be complete. It must also be complete if there are differences in evaluation arising from the risk and uncertainty involved. However, for the bilateral-monopoly problem encountered in licensing an advantage, control is not always necessary; a profit-sharing plan (for example, a minority interest) will often be sufficient. If both parties receive a constant share of profits, there is no conflict over what is to be maximized, and the distortion effects of charging a price for the license in excess of marginal cost (which in the case of a license is zero) do not arise.

Dunning[3] has found some interesting aspects of the determinants of form. He finds that United States firms sometimes relinquish part of the control of their United Kingdom subsidiaries as a condition of borrowing from

[3] J. H. Dunning, American Investment in British Manufacturing Industry (London: George Allen and Unwin Ltd., 1958).

British sources.[4] This is just one case of a more general rule; parent firms often share control of their
foreign subsidiaries if there are other firms or persons who have something to contribute to the operation.
This rule is also seen in another finding of Dunning's;
the more similar the product structures of the parent
and the subsidiary, the more the control; the greater
the necessity for local adaptation, the less the control.[5]

The way in which form is related to the underlying
relationship is a fascinating and important study. The
"firm" is a particular form of relating various activities in the economy. A study of the determinants of the
forms of international operations could probably tell
much about the nature of the firm and help clarify the
theory of the firm. But little is known.

The Manysidedness of International Operations
We began this study by trying to explain the flow of
direct investment. In order to do this, we were led to
study the international operations of firms. The most
important aspect of international operations may be the

[4]Ibid., p. 98.
[5]Ibid.

capital flows associated with them, but it is by no means the only aspect. Also associated with international operations is the flow of business technique and skilled personnel.

The data on these aspects are very meager. All we know of this migration of men is that there are 9,000 American citizens employed in Latin America by American companies.[6] About the flow of business technique we know almost nothing. The payments for the skills of the parent firm are included in the profits it receives from its foreign subsidiary or associate. Empirically, it is not possible to separate that part of the return which is the interest on capital and that part which is payment for other services rendered.

The term "technical assistance" is not used for good reason. We presented as one theoretical motivation for control, the monopoly control of the industry. Whether the increased profits which result from the control of price and output in this connection should be classified as technical assistance is doubtful. Something similar

[6]U.S. Department of Commerce, Office of Business Economics, U.S. Investments in the Latin American Economy (Washington: U.S. Government Printing Office, 1957), p. 122.

may be true of other functions as well.

We concentrate on capital movements because of the historical tradition and because more is known about them than anything else. But they are, after all, only one dimension of a much broader phenomenon. When we try to measure the extent of international operations for the purpose of testing hypotheses or determining effects, it is not the only measure we could use and perhaps not the appropriate one.

If we had the information, we could use the portion of a country's GNP represented by the value added of enterprises under foreign control. This would not completely cover international operations; the difficulty of determining the extent of control and deciding which types of control should be included is formidable. In particular, we would be leaving out licensing agreements and management contracts, which are an important part of international operations. Instead of value added, we could use assets as an index of international operations. This measure is subject to the same limitations as value added plus an additional one. It assumes that capital is a measure of size and thus ignores other factors of production. Direct investment is further removed from the ideal measure. It is sub-

ject to variations arising from differences in methods
of finance.

Another measure would be the annual flow between
nations of certain services connected with foreign operations. This measure would include interest, profit,
wages of foreigners, royalties, and consultant fees.
There may be a case for including the value of exports
as well. One shortcoming of this measure is the fact
that to some extent an American firm will increase its
profits in the United States by having foreign operations (as, for example, when the acquisition of a foreign enterprise removes the competition of imports).
This increase will not be measured by the firm's income from abroad. This is an important thing to consider because one of the reasons for foreign operations
is the jointness of profits of the enterprises at home
and the enterprises abroad.[7]

In empirical work you make use of what you have.
For the most part we shall use direct investment as a
measure of international operations, and we shall supplement it with other indexes where possible. One of

[7]It also implies that it would be very difficult to measure the profitability on foreign direct investments.

the purposes of the analysis of the last chapter was to
indicate the theoretical connections between the various measures, and these should be kept in mind in any
discussion of a particular problem of international operations.

The International Distribution of Advantages and the
Role of Historical Accident

At least some (and more likely most) international operations are due to the unequal ability of firms to conduct a certain activity. To explain international operations, therefore, it is important to know this distribution of ability. But we know very little about the ability
of firms. A good deal of what we know is contained in
Bain's analysis of barriers to entry, and that deals
with only twenty industries and only in the United States.[8]
In the absence of detailed information it is worthwhile
examining some general features.

Why do firms of different countries have unequal
ability? In part it is due to the fact that there is an unequal distribution of skills among people. The popula-
tion of every country is a sample of the universe, and

[8] J. S. Bain, Barriers to New Competition (Cambridge,
Mass.: Harvard University Press, 1956).

the particular distribution of skills will vary from country to country for no other reason than this. In part it
is also due to the chance discovery of a gold mine, a
valuable formula, or Scotch whiskey. If this were all
there was, there would not be much interest in analyz-
ing the direction of the flow of international operations.
The problem becomes interesting only when the distribution of advantages is systematically unequal between
countries. Then we can analyze why some countries
have more international operations than others.

One would expect that firms in relatively advanced
countries would in general have advantages over firms
in less developed countries, but it is not always true,
and historical accident may also be involved. In the
relatively advanced and rich countries there are more
skilled personnel and better developed capital markets.
By itself this does not give firms of the advanced countries an advantage over firms of less developed countries. They have the advantage because they have better
access to these factors of production for reasons discussed before, that is, that there are reasonable and
unreasonable preferences by employees and investors
for companies of their own country.

Developed countries provide a better training ground

for entrepreneurs. They have industries that poor countries do not have, and the firms in these industries are
likely to be national firms. By operating in these industries, the firms have an opportunity gradually to
acquire experience and achieve size. They become
"established" firms, with advantages over nationals of
less developed countries.

This hypothesis, that the firms which have advantages
are more likely to be from advanced countries than from
less developed countries, is consistent with the observed
fact that the major exporters of direct investment are
and have been the well-developed countries of Europe
and, of course, the United States. It is interesting in
this context to ask what will happen with time in a particular country to the share of industry controlled by
foreigners.[9] There is no single answer: there are some
forces which increase the advantages of foreigners
over local firms and some forces which decrease them;
which set of forces predominates in a particular industry is a question which can be decided only by de-

[9]To avoid misunderstanding, it must be stressed that
although this is an important question to the economist
interested in the behavior of the economy, it is not necessarily of any relevance to policy considerations.

tailed study. Tending to encourage the entry of local
firms are the following: (1) as the country develops,
the supply of local skilled persons and capital increases;
(2) as the market grows, whatever barriers were introduced by economies of scale diminish in importance;
(3) there is a demonstration effect—the existence of
profits induces local firms to follow the example and
enter the industry. There are also forces which tend
to make it more difficult for local firms to enter. The
foreign firms operating in the industry may find their
advantages increasing relative to new national firms
through growing product differentiation, continuing research, and increasing access to factors of production.
The foreign firms become even more "established."

The fact that advantages may increase brings up the
question of how much historical accident is involved in
international operations. Suppose a firm has an advantage and is considering establishing a foreign operation. It decides not to, perhaps because of a bad ad-
ministrative decision. In the absence of its activity in
the foreign country, a local firm begins operations.
Then years later the local firm may be an established
firm, and it may no longer be profitable for the original firm to change its mind and establish a foreign subsidiary.

This consideration of historical accident comes into
play whenever it is true that a firm's ability in a given
year depends on its past activity. It may be important,
and the problem arises when we consider the distribution of United States investments. It is well known that
the share of United States industry in Latin America
is greater than the share of United States industry in
Europe.[10] Is this because Europe is richer than Latin
America, and will it disappear as Latin America develops? It is hard to tell because Europe is both richer
and older than Latin America. But in Canada we have
a country that is both rich and young. The share of
America in Canadian manufacturing, for example, is
very high and in recent years has been increasing.[11]
Canada has as large an automobile industry as Italy,
yet there is no Canadian automobile firm. But Canada
is not really a good test case because of its geographi-
cal and cultural proximity to the United States. Unfortunately there are no good cases which can discrim-

[10] To some extent this is illustrated in Table 3.1.

[11] See Dominion Bureau of Statistics, International Trade
Division, Balance of Payments Section, Canada's Inter-
national Investment Position 1926-1954 (Ottawa: Queen's
Printer and Controller of Stationery, 1958), p. 91.

Table 3.1 National Income and United States Direct Investment by Area (millions of dollars)

Area	1953 National Income	1950 U.S. Direct Investment	
		All Industries	Manufacturing
Canada	19,482	3,579	1,897
Latin America	40,412	4,735	780
Western Europe	162,494	1,720	932
Australia and New Zealand	10,111	226	107
Other non-Communist areas	90,926	1,528	116

Sources: 1. M. H. Watkins, Estimate of World Income, 1953 (Cambridge, Mass.: Center for International Studies, M. I. T., 1956)
2. U.S. Department of Commerce, Office of Business Economics, Direct Private Foreign Investments of the United States (Washington: U.S. Government Printing Office, 1953), p. 44.

inate between the various forces which influence the
pattern of international operations.[12] But it is an interesting question as to how much history is involved,
and perhaps also an important one.

In the United States, as growth occurred, many for-
eign-owned enterprises were taken over by Americans.
But the war helped this process (through seizure of
German assets by the United States government, and
the forced sale of some British assets by the United
Kingdom government), and the experience may be
unique. The rayon industry is an interesting case of
both economic forces and history at work. Every profitable rayon venture in the United States began with
some type of association with European firms.[13] As
rayon technology in the United States reached the level
of that in Europe, however, domestic firms began to

[12] Australia and New Zealand are like Canada in that
they are young and rich and English-speaking. Unlike
Canada, they are not geographically close to the United
States. As Table 3.1 shows, the ratio of American investment to their national income is higher than for
Europe. Further study of these countries might be useful.

[13] J. W. Markham, Competition in the Rayon Industry
(Cambridge, Mass.: Harvard University Press, 1952),
pp. 20, 21.

break away from their parent or affiliated European
companies.[14] But the break was helped by the Second
World War, during which time several German subsidiaries were taken over by the United States government and the ownership of American Viscose was sold
by Courtaulds.

In England, Dunning questioned 115 United States-
controlled firms and found that for the period 1939 to
1954, sixty-three firms claimed their share of the
market had increased, thirty-seven claimed it had remained constant, and fifteen claimed their share de-
creased.[15] This shows that anything can happen. From
the point of view of historical accident, the following
quotation is relevant:

The tendency for a subsidiary to develop independent
of the parent concern and, in consequence, for relationships between the two companies to become distinct,
was greatly accelerated by the war, during which time
such subsidiaries not only came under the control of
British natives, but evolved separate product lines of
their own.

International Operations and International Trade

The industries in which international operations occur

[14]Ibid., pp. 20, 21, 209.

[15]Dunning, American Investment in British Manufacturing Industry, p. 184.

are often industries in which international trade was
or is important. The international operations frequently
were established to replace exports or to produce imports. Some empirical evidence on this association of
trade with international operation is available. The
United States Department of Commerce reports that in
1956, 23 percent of all United States imports came from
United States-controlled enterprises operating in foreign countries.[16] Of the total sales of United States
companies operating in Latin America, 43 percent was
for export, a good part of it to the United States.[17] In
England, too, international trade is an important activity of United States subsidiaries. Dunning found that
though the American firms in his sample accounted for

[16]S. Pizer and F. Cutler, "Growth of Foreign Investments in the United States and Abroad," Survey of Current Business, XXXVI (August 1956), p. 24. The percent was more than twice as high in the selected commodities (accounting for slightly less than half of total
imports) in which international operations occur.

[17]U.S. Department of Commerce, Office of Business
Economics, U.S. Investments in the Latin American
Economy, p. 113. As one would expect, the percent
exported is higher for mining and smelting (86 percent),
agriculture (80 percent), and petroleum (52 percent),
and lower for manufacturing (6 percent) and public utilities (1 percent).

less than 3 percent of the total number of employees
in British manufacturing industries, they accounted
for 12 percent of manufacturing exports.[18]

There is good theoretical reason for this close association between international trade and international
operations. In some cases, international operations
occur only because there is actual or potential trade.
Trade brings the enterprises of one country into contact with the enterprises of another country; this contact often causes conflict, and international operations
are one means of resolving this conflict. There is also
a close association between trade and advantages. Advantages can be thought of as factors of production. If
a firm possesses an advantage in a certain activity, it
is likely to export the commodity which embodies its
advantages. When there is a change in cost conditions
and it becomes profitable to produce abroad, this firm

[18]Dunning, American Investment in British Manufacturing Industry, pp. 58, 295. The type of exporting
done by American firms in England is very different
from the exporting done by firms in Latin America. In
Latin America it is mostly a matter of exporting raw
materials to the United States and elsewhere. In England, the firms are in manufacturing industries, and
their exports are a replacement or a substitute for exports from the parent company.

may establish the foreign operations, for it still has its advantages.[19] Not only do the advantages lead to trade, but trade may lead to advantages, for through its export activities a firm may establish distribution channels or may establish a differentiated product.

This brings up the infant-industry argument, which is really an infant-firm argument. It never pays to put a tariff on because the market is small, for it will result only in raising the price and making the market smaller. The thing to do is to wait until the market is large enough to support an optimum-sized plant. Then perhaps a tariff may serve as a catalyst. The tariff argument may, however, apply to an infant firm. The infant firm, in the frame of reference of our study, is a firm which is at a disadvantage but which would overcome the disadvantage through time. There is one trouble. The imposition of a tariff may result in the foreign firm's establishing a subsidiary. The local firm may then never get started—much less established.

[19]An interesting sidelight on this point is found in the 1950 annual report of the Caterpillar Tractor Company. The report offers as one reason for the establishment of a foreign subsidiary, "The growth of foreign business in spurious parts in place of genuine Caterpillar parts." (Underlining supplied.)

The ability of firms to substitute international operations for exports lost has implications for the balance of payments. Dollar shortages have probably had
two opposing effects on American investment. Exchange restrictions and depreciations, actual and expected, tended to discourage investment. But the loss
of foreign markets due to the very same exchange-rate
problems tended to increase the profitability of going
abroad.[20]

Block considered only the first effect and said that
the dollar shortage had blocked the very investment
which would alleviate it. As proof, he pointed out that
much of the direct investment since the war has been
dollar-oriented, that is, went into the production of
materials for sale to dollar countries or other hard-
currency areas. As he put it, "the obstacles to direct
investment are those obstacles arising from the dollar
shortage."[21] But at the same time there was much

---

[20]This is aside from the exchange restrictions which
prevented foreign firms from taking money out of a
country, thus giving them no alternative but to invest
it there.

[21]E. Block, "United States Foreign Investment and the
Dollar Shortage," The Review of Economics and Statistics, XXXV (May 1953), p. 154.

soft-currency-oriented investment in manufacturing
for local sales in Latin America. True manufacturing
investment did not increase as fast as direct investment in oil. But very few things ever grew as fast as
investment in oil. And the fact that much investment
goes to Canada is nothing new; this was true in the
twenties, when the dollar shortage was not an important fact in investment decisions.

The annual reports of Johnson and Johnson provide
an interesting example of the two effects. The literary
part of the annual reports are replete with complaints
of foreign governmental control, exchange trouble,
unfavorable business climate abroad, and so forth.
The reports are, in fact, almost a model list of obstacles to direct investment. However, the statements
at the front of the annual reports do not prepare the
reader for the figures at the back which show that the
direct investment of Johnson and Johnson amounted to
$8 million in 1946, $15 million in 1950, and $29 mil-
lion in 1957.

We have not discussed the association between direct
investment and trade in the usual manner which dis-
tinguishes three relations: (1) where the direct investment increases exports, (2) where the direct invest-

ment decreases imports, (3) where the direct investment does neither.

We have not treated the relation in this way because
of the great difficulties involved in discovering the effect. Every investment affects the production-possibil-
ity curve of a country and the distribution of income
and therefore demand. What the final impact on trade
will be may have little connection with what happens in
a particular industry. As an example of the difficulty,
consider the following case. An American firm invests
in a foreign country in an industry which exports. Does
this mean the investment is export-increasing? Suppose
the reason for the international operations was to obtain
market control and to restrict output in some places. It
is then possible that if the American firm had not made
the investment and if, instead, a local firm had made
it, trade would be greater. We have to distinguish carefully what we are comparing. We may compare what
happens if the American makes the investment to what
would happen if the investment was not made at all. Or
the relevant comparison might be with what would happen
if it were made by someone else.

Monopoly and International Operations

Monopoly problems pervade any discussion of international operations and direct investment.

For example, in the preceding discussion, there was continual mention of indeterminacy arising from oligopoly problems. In any policy discussion of direct investment, one also finds that part of the debate is meaningful only if it is analyzed in terms of imperfections and impurities of the market. Foreign firms are accused of controlling the industry, of exploiting labor or consumers, of being too big, and of being too profitable. These are exactly the same charges found in the politics of antitrust, except now there is additional passion, for the object of attack is a foreigner.

Both in theory and in fact, where international operations occur, considerations of perfect competition are not likely to apply. The theoretical points in support of this were made in Chapter 2 and will only be summarized here. The empirical support will be presented in Chapter 4. The first major cause of international operations given in Chapter 2 was the removal of conflict between enterprises in different countries which either sell to each other or sell in the same market. This conflict stems from the impurities of the market and would not arise in competitive industries. The second major cause of international operations was

the exploitation of an advantage. In this case the firm
usually has the alternative of licensing the advantage
instead of itself establishing foreign operations. It will
be recalled that many of the reasons for choosing not
to license arose from the imperfect nature of the market for the advantage. These imperfections prevented
the appropriation of all the returns to the advantage.
When, on the other hand, there are many buyers of
the advantage, many of the reasons for establishing a
foreign subsidiary disappear, and the alternative of
licensing becomes more attractive.

There is also a presumption that the kinds of abilities
which lead to international operations will most often
be possessed by only a few firms. If many firms possess this ability, then it is probably not too difficult
to acquire. Local firms will then be able to acquire it,
and since they have special advantages in their own
country because of their nationality, they (and not foreign firms) are likely to predominate in this industry.
The exception to this occurs in very underdeveloped
countries. In less developed countries, the natives may
be so lacking in ability that they would not be able to
compete successfully in industries which in advanced
countries are nearly perfectly competitive, for example,

farming. Foreigners may then operate in these industries even though there are many firms in the industry.
Another example is the case where large projects in a
small country are financed in large capital markets because that amount of capital cannot be raised locally.
There still may be many such projects and a competitive industry.

The association of oligopoly elements with international operations is important in two respects. The
first is that it introduces a certain degree of indeterminacy into the extent of international operations. Repeated instances of this were encountered in the discussion of the theory of international operations, and
they will be encountered in any empirical investigation.
An interesting and illustrative example of these problems can be found in the following two case studies of
events in the early part of this century.

In the nineteenth century the United States exported
meat to Great Britain and Europe. The advent of re-
frigerated shipping made it economical for Europe to
switch its imports from United States to Latin America.
Both British and American firms established meat-
packing plants in Latin America. A bitter battle re-

sulted, but firms of both countries remained in the industry.[22]

Contrast this with the tobacco case. Here is Dunning's description.

. . . at the turn of the century, the British tobacco industry was literally "invaded" by American capital.
Restricted in its sales by a high tariff wall imposed
on U.S. cigarettes, the American Tobacco Company
acquired the young and prosperous firm of Ogdens,
Ltd., in September 1901, and straight away launched
an extensive publicity campaign to sell cheap cigarettes. The Chairman of the U.S. company at that time
made no secret of his intentions, viz.: "to obtain a
large share of the tobacco trade both of England and
the Continent," and he threatened to spend up to £ 6
million in doing just this. The reaction of the British
producers was prompt for within a month of the purchase of Ogden's, thirteen of the leading tobacco companies had amalgamated and formed themselves into
Imperial Tobacco Company, with an issued capital of
£ 14 1/2 million. Then followed several months of cut
throat competition between the two concerns. . . .
Eventually, a market sharing agreement was reached
in September 1902; Ogden's became part of the Imperial Tobacco group, which was given the monopoly
of the British and Irish markets, whilst the United
States and its dependencies were to be supplied by the
American Tobacco Company. A new concern, the

[22]L. Corey, Meat and Man (New York: The Viking
Press, 1950), pp. 202-206.

British-American Tobacco Co., Ltd., was set up to
handle the remainder of the export business and was
allocated factories both in the United States and in the
United Kingdom. . . .[23]

The second important implication of the oligopolistic

nature of international operation is in the area of policy.

This will not be discussed here. Instead, one general

point will be made. Because of the oligopolistic nature

there is room for bargaining. The firm will often be

receiving a return above its opportunity costs on the

services it provides for its international operations.

It is possible for foreign governments to tax these

rents without affecting behavior. This is not a policy

prescription, but to the observer it is interesting to

study the negotiations between firms and governments

in this bilateral-monopoly situation.[24]

---

[23] Dunning, American Investment in British Manufacturing Industry, pp. 30-31.

[24] An analysis of these problems (and especially of the
50-50 partnership solution) is found in C. P. Kindle-
berger, International Economics (Homewood, Ill.:
Richard D. Irwin, Inc., 2d ed., 1958), pp. 402-406.
For a recent description see E. T. Penrose, "Profit
Sharing Between Producing Countries and Oil Compa-
nies in the Middle East," The Economic Journal, LXIX
(June 1959), p. 238.

Summary

The discussion in this chapter has been long, and it is
appropriate here to summarize in systematic fashion
the points considered. We have stated that international
operations occur only under special conditions; that
when they occur, many forms are possible; and that it
is not always possible to predict precisely the form or
the extent of international operations because of the
monopolistic nature of the markets in which they evolve.
We proceed with the summary by discussing various
types of industries where international operations occur, some of the factors which determine the form,
and the nature of the indeterminacy involved. We distinguish four pure cases. In actual industries there
will be a mixture of the pure cases.

1. International operations will occur in those industries in which enterprises of different countries sell
in the same market or sell to each other under conditions of imperfect competition. The form will vary;
there may be collusion, tacit or overt; the enterprises
may merge and become one firm; they may have a
profit-sharing agreement (through minority interests,
for example); for a time the enterprises may even compete. But if there is interdependence and if there are

only a few firms so that they can recognize this interdependence, some form of accommodation will eventually occur. In an empirical investigation we would
look for concentrated industries in which there is international trade. The pattern of international operations will be determined by the pattern of trade. Between countries that trade, there will be international
operations; between countries that do not trade, there
will be none.

2. International operations will also occur in industries
where some firms have advantages over other firms.
There are several subcases:

   The rarest case will be the one where there is a
single firm which has advantages over all other firms
in the world in the production of a particular product
through, for example, its possession of a strong patent. Wherever the product is produced, the firm will
have some part in its production. Its part, however,
can range from a licensing agreement to complete control, and it need not be the same in all countries. When
the patent can be most efficiently used by many enterprises, licensing is likely to be the chosen method. If,
on the other hand, industry conditions are such that
there will be only one or a few enterprises in each mar-

ket, a stronger form of control is more likely. The
method chosen will depend partly on the firm's position at a particular point of time; for example, if it is
expanding rapidly and is short of capital, it may resort
to a looser form of control in order to raise capital in
the country of operations. The form will also depend
on the particular country involved. In those countries
where there are strong discriminations against foreigners or where there are local firms with comple-
mentary skills, some form of cooperation will be likely;
the relinquishment of control will be compensated for
by the decrease in costs.

A more prevalent case of international operations
occurs in industries where there is not just one firm
but several firms with advantages. However, it is not
likely that there will be many firms. For if there are
many firms, entry is probably easy, and local firms
with the special advantages of their nationality will
predominate. The exception to this proposition will
occur in those countries where the nationals are so
poor that they cannot survive in any industry.

The several firms with advantages may not all be of
the same country. Capable firms can arise in many
countries because entrepreneurs are born everywhere

and because the history of the world is that until re-
cently economics were quite separate and firms could
develop in isolated home markets.

There is no single solution when there are a few
firms. The firms will differ slightly among themselves,
and their pattern of development will reflect this. More
important, there may be some cases of market sharing.
The national firms might predominate in their own market, and they might divide up the rest of the world into
spheres of influence. Or they might compete in each
and every market, including their home markets. In
our present state of knowledge, an indeterminacy is
involved where oligopoly matters are concerned. This
is very important when an attempt is made to explain
direct investment. Direct investment is associated
with international operations—whatever indeterminacy
there is in the one, there also must be in the other.
3. The third case of international operations arises
from interdependence of enterprises in different countries other than the two reasons (market impurity and
unequal ability) just presented. One such interdependence comes about from the fact that profits in one country may be negatively correlated with profits of another
country; when one goes up, the other goes down. Or the

profits may be independent. In either case an investor
may be able to achieve greater stability in his profits
by diversifying his portfolio and investing part in each
country. This investment may be undertaken by shareholders of the firm, and not the firm itself, and no control may be involved. It will probably depend on who
has the better resources for acquiring information.

Reasons other than diversification may be causes of
interdependence and international operations. I do not
know of any that are empirically important, but doubt-
lessly they exist and will be uncovered by further research.

4. The fourth and last case is the case where international operations do not occur. Industries of this kind
probably account for the preponderant share of the
gross national product of countries. Industries with
many small firms are likely to fall into this category,
although even here isolated cases of international operations are possible depending on the peculiar circumstances of individual firms. Industries with no international operations predominate partly because of
purely economic facts and partly because of the lack
of integration in the world economy. The greater the
nationalism, the greater the disparity in ability neces-

sary to cause international operations. There is a vi-
cious circle involved. For the greater the nationalism,
the greater the profits must be in local currency, and
this leads to greater hostility to foreign "exploitation."
This concludes the summary. In the next chapter we
shall present a survey of empirical evidence which illustrates the arguments we have just made.

4
SOME EMPIRICAL EVIDENCE ON UNITED STATES INTERNATIONAL OPERATIONS—MAINLY IN MANUFACTURING INDUSTRIES

Introduction

The theory of international operations just presented may be plausible, and it may be valid, but it certainly makes the task of empirical investigation exceedingly difficult. The theory implies that the relevant units of study are particular industries and particular firms and not the aggregates of international operations. This type of information is simply not available. To make a proper study of international operations, one would need to know the industrial composition of national product for each country, the share of industry output in each country of firms of every nationality, the strength of the advantages of firms, and details of the structure of industries and the patterns of international trade. What we have is considerably less. The United States is the only major direct-investing country which regularly publishes reasonably complete and consistent data on its foreign investments. Even here the investment data are broken down only into broad industrial categories. It is usually not possible to estimate the United States share of production in other countries, because for most industries total output by industry is not known. About the advantages of individual firms, almost no independent measure is available.

One can make some headway by studying individual
firms and industries. But the way is treacherous. When
there is little solid basis of information, any precon-
ceived pattern can be supported by observed behavior,
and individual detailed studies still remain special
cases.

What follows is a survey of such information as is
available on United States participation in manufacturing industries in foreign countries. Most of the data
is taken from government publications or from the few
empirical studies which have been made. These data,
taken as a whole, suggest some simple propositions
which are consistent with the discussion of the last two
chapters and which illustrate some of the hypotheses.

Three of the main features suggested by the survey
are: (1) that American foreign operations are concentrated in a few industries and are conducted by a com-
paratively small number of firms; (2) that in these industries, United States companies account for a large
and often major share of the output in foreign countries; (3) that often in these same industries where
American firms have substantial foreign operations,
one of the firms operating in the United States is a foreign firm. This concentration in certain industries, the

predominance of American firms in these industries,
and the existence of cross investment are consistent
with the prediction of the theory of international operations presented in the last chapter.

The other important feature of international operations is its association with concentrated industries.
International operations of United States firms seldom
occur in industries where there is a large number of
firms. Moreover, the firms that have international
operations are large at home, and their subsidiaries
are large abroad. Large size and concentration are by
no means the same thing, but they are empirically related.

The reader may be warned of two biases in the presentation that follows. The studies of international operations from which the data are taken were not designed with the propositions just mentioned in mind.
Had they been so designed, the illustrations might be
clearer and more striking. On the other hand, these
sources were read by me with the propositions very
much in mind, and the selection of evidence to be presented here is, no doubt, biased on this account.
Partly in an attempt to guard against this latter fault,
I have made liberal use of direct quotations from the
texts dealing with the subject.

Aggregate United States Investment

In this section some statistical evidence on the following points is presented:

1. Certain United States industries have significantly
more foreign investment than other industries. In later
sections we try to show that those industries which have
much investment are industries in which the share of
United States firms is high throughout the world.

2. A few firms in a few industries account for a substantial portion of United States direct investment.

3. The industries in which there is much foreign investment tend to be concentrated industries, while the
industries in which there is little or no foreign investment tend to be unconcentrated.

4. Most of the investing is done by large firms.

5. In at least ten industries in which United States
firms have foreign investments, one of the leading
firms operating in the United States is a foreign firm.

It should be stressed that the data to be presented
are very poor and only suggest these five propositions
rather than in any sense prove them.

Industrial Distribution   Table 4.1 shows the industrial
distribution of United States direct investment as compared to the industrial distribution of the total assets

Table 4.1 Foreign Investment and Total Assets of United
States Companies, 1950, by Industry (millions of dollars)

	Foreign Investments of U.S. Companies	Total Assets of All Companies in the U.S.	Foreign Assets as a Percent of Total Assets in the U.S.[a]
	(1)	(2)	(3)
Products of petroleum and coal	3,390[b]	17,439[b]	19.4
All manufacturing, excluding petroleum and coal	3,831[c]	93,856	4.1
Rubber products	182	2,053	8.9
Paper and allied products	378	4,515	8.4
Electrical machinery, equipment, and supplies	386	4,691	8.2
Motor vehicles and equipment	485	8,153	6.1
Chemicals and allied products	513	9,659	5.3
Machinery (except electrical)	420	9,546	4.4
Food products	483	12,198	4.0
All other manufacturing*	599	25,124	2.4
Primary and fabricated metals	385	17,897	2.1

*All other manufacturing
  refers to the following:

Tobacco manufactures	n.a.	2,362
Textile mill products	n.a.	6,132
Apparel and finished textiles	n.a.	1,554

Table 4.1   Foreign Investment and Total Assets of United
States Companies, 1950, by Industry (millions of dollars)
(continued)

	Foreign Investments of U.S. Companies	Total Assets of All Companies in the U.S.	Foreign Assets as a Percent of Total Assets in the U.S.[a]
Lumber and wood products	n. a.	2,069	
Furniture and fixtures	n. a.	934	
Printing and publishing, except newspapers	n. a.	2,081	
Leather and leather products	n. a.	985	
Stone, clay, and glass products	n. a.	3,306	
Instruments: photographic and optical goods, watches and clocks	n. a.	1,515	
Transportation equipment except motor vehicles	n. a.	2,630	
Miscellaneous manufacturing industries, including ordnance	n. a.	1,556	

Note: n. a. means not available.

[a]There exists considerable discrepancy between the definition
of Column 1 and that of Column 2, and in some unknown cases,
total assets of Column 2 include some foreign assets. It is
therefore not particularly meaningful to derive the percent figures in Column 3. They should be interpreted as an index of
the ranking of industries with respect to importance of foreign
investment rather than as actual percentages.

[b]Total assets of all companies in the United States in the petroleum industry include products of coal. Foreign investments

Table 4.1 Foreign Investment and Total Assets of United
States Companies, 1950, by Industry (millions of dollars)
(continued)

of this industry include nonmanufacturing operations but do not
include products of coal.

cExcludes manufacturing operations of mining companies.
Sources: Column 1. U.S. Department of Commerce, Office of
Business Economics, Direct Private Foreign Investments of
the United States, Census of 1950 (Washington: U.S. Govern-
ment Printing Office, 1953), p. 44.
Column 2. U.S. Federal Trade Commission and U.S. Securi-
ties and Exchange Commission, Quarterly Industrial Financial
Report Series—For All United States Manufacturing Corpora-
tions, First Quarter 1950 (Washington: U.S. Government
Printing Office, 1950).

of all firms in the United States. By no means is the

distribution of foreign investments equal among indus-

tries. Relative to total assets, foreign investment is

high in petroleum, rubber, paper, electrical equip-

ment, motor vehicles, and machinery, while it is low

for other industries. However, the industrial catego-

ries used are very broad, and a finer breakdown might

reveal other industries where foreign investment is

high relative to domestic assets.

A more detailed industry breakdown is presented in

Table 4.2, but it is based on less reliable data. The

information in Table 4.1 is based on census data, which

Table 4.2 Income from Foreign Sources[a] as a Percent of Net Income[b] for Manufacturing Companies as Reported to the United States Treasury Department, Average of Years: 1950, 1951, 1954, 1955

	Income from Foreign Sources as Percent of Net Income[c]
Petroleum and coal products	21.80
Rubber products	10.52
Chemical and allied products	3.67
Food and kindred products	3.62
Motor vehicles and equipment, except electrical	3.28
Scientific instruments, photographic equipment, watches and clocks	3.00
Stone, clay and glass products	2.63
Primary metal industries	2.65
Fabricated metal products, except ordnance, machinery and transportation equipment	2.42
Electrical machinery and equipment	2.29
Machinery, except transportation equipment and electrical	2.14
Paper and allied products	2.10
Transportation equipment except motor vehicles	1.62
Printing, publishing, and allied industries	1.45
Furniture and fixtures	1.17
Other manufacturing	1.10
Beverages	.89
Textiles—mill products	.54
Apparel and products made from fabrics	.54
Tobacco manufactures	.46
Ordnance and accessories	.34
Leather and products	.30
Lumber and wood products, except furniture	.17

Table 4.2 Income from Foreign Sources[a] as a Percent of Net
Income[b] for Manufacturing Companies as Reported to the
United States Treasury Department, Average of Years:
1950, 1951, 1954, 1955 (continued)

[a]"Income from Foreign Sources" refers to income reported by
firms filing statements (Form 1118) in support of credit claimed
for foreign taxes paid.

[b]"Net Income" refers to net income before tax for all returns.

[c]As in Table 4.1, these numbers are best thought of as indexes
of rank rather than actual percentages.

Source: Calculated from data published annually by the Internal
Revenue Service of the U.S. Treasury Department in Statistics
of Income, Part 2, Corporation Income Tax Returns. Years
used were 1950, 1951, 1954, and 1955.

are reasonably complete. The information in Table 4.2

is based on Statistics of Income data which cover only

those firms which claimed credit for foreign taxes and

which filed statements to support their claim.[1] The in-

dustrial classification also differs somewhat from

Table 4.1 to Table 4.2. The census classifies invest-

ment on the basis of the activity of the foreign firm,

whereas the Treasury Department makes the classifi-

cation on the basis of the recipient's activity. The other

main difference between the two tables is that in Table

4.1 the data refer to assets, while in Table 4.2 they

[1]Some idea of the coverage of statistics of income data can be obtained from the following data for 1950:

Net earnings on all United States direct investments (Census)	$1,765,900
Net receipts of income from direct investments (Census)	1,293,600
Retained earnings of foreign subsidiaries (Census)	$ 472,300
Net foreign income of all firms reported in Statistics of Income	$1,334,101

Source: U.S. Department of Commerce, Office of Business Economics, Direct Private Foreign Investments of
the United States, Census of 1950 (Washington: U.S.
Government Printing Office, 1953), p. 35; and U.S.
Treasury Department, Internal Revenue Service, Statistics of Income for 1950, Part 2 (Washington: U.S.
Government Printing Office, 1954), p. 44.

refer to income. Because income is more subject to transitory fluctuations than are assets, an average of four years, 1950, 1951, 1954, and 1955, was used for Table 4.2. There is no particular significance in the selection of dates to be omitted except that information on income from foreign sources was not published for 1952.

Despite the lack of comparability of the data for the two tables, the pattern is similar. The data in Table 4.2 are arranged in order of percentage of income derived from foreign sources. The skew is again evident, and the order is not very different from that of Table 4.1. Petroleum, rubber, chemicals, and motor vehicles are again high, while textiles, apparel, tobacco, ordnance, leather, and lumber are low. There are some exceptions: food, primary metals, and fabricated metals are higher than machinery, except electrical, and electrical machinery, whereas in Table 4.1 they were lower. There is also some new information: some of the subcategories of "all other manufacturing" of Table 4.1 rank high on the list (for example, scientific instruments).

The Major Investing Firms   Both of these tables underestimate the unevenness of the distribution of foreign operations because both tables deal with fairly broad

and somewhat heterogeneous industrial categories. It
is difficult to obtain data on finer industry classifications, but some indication is given by the fact that a
good portion of American direct investment is made by
only a few firms (as illustrated in Table 4.3). In fact,
of the $3.39 billion of foreign investment in oil, $3.124
billion was accounted for by seven firms. In other manufacturing, the facts are not quite so dramatic but nevertheless still impressive. Total direct investment in
manufacturing (excluding petroleum) was $3.83 billion.
Eleven firms with direct investments of over $50 mil-
lion accounted for $1.373 billion, or over a third, while
another sixteen firms with investments between $26
and $50 million had investments of $595 million, bringing the total of the top twenty-seven investors, with
foreign investments of $25 million or more, to $1.968
billion, or about half of the total.

Since a few firms account for so much and since these
firms are in only a few industries, it is to be expected
that a finer industrial breakdown would show even more
unevenness in the distribution of foreign investments
than was shown in Tables 4.1 and 4.2. Table 4.3 shows
which manufacturing industries the twenty-seven large
foreign investors are in. It is possible to guess at the

identity of these firms by examining annual reports,
but it is not possible to know with certainty. Not all
firms publish data on their foreign activities. Those
that do publish do not necessarily do so in a consistent
fashion.

Food The five large investors in the food industry with
foreign investments of over $25 million are probably
International Packers, the Corn Products Refining Company, the Coca-Cola Company, Swift and Company, and
Armour and Company. Two other firms, the H. J.
Heinz Company and Wilson and Company, appear to
have close to $25 million. International Packers may
very well have over $50 million in assets.

The importance of meat packing in the foreign investments of the food industry is here evident and is supported by the fact that of the $235 million of United
States investment in Argentina, Brazil, Uruguay, and
Chile in branch plant operations in 1932, $95 million,
or nearly one half, was in meat packing.[2] The meat-
packing industry, though not now highly concentrated,

[2]See Table 4.12 and D. M. Phelps, Migration of Industry to South America (New York: McGraw-Hill Book
Company, Inc., 1936), p. 24.

Table 4.3 Distribution of Foreign Investments by Industry and
Size Categories, 1950 (millions of dollars)

| | Companies Having Foreign Investments[a] (in millions of dollars) of: | | | |
| | 1-5 | | 6-25 | |
Industry	No. of Companies	Value of Investments	No. of Companies	Value of Investments
Petroleum	10	27	9[c]	129
Manufacturing, total	192	439	79	1,010
Food	9	25	17	212
Paper products	12	25	5	70
Chemical	21	43	14	170
Primary and fabricated metals	25	54	7[c]	124
Machinery	34	78	11	137
Automotive and electrical	26	60	9	121
Other	65	154	16	176

[a]The individual firm data were compiled by the Office of Business Economics of the Department of Commerce from the Census of Direct Foreign Investment of 1950. The complete survey covered 442 firms (the data presented here are only those for manufacturing and petroleum), each with foreign investments of $1 million or more. These 442 firms account for

Over 25		Total: All Companies[a]		Total of 1950 Census[b]
No. of Com- panies	Value of Invest- ments	No. of Com- panies	Value of Invest- ments	Value of Invest- ments
7	3,124	26	3,280	3,390
27[e]	1,968	298	3,417	3,831
5	209	31	446	483
4	209	21	304	378
4	174	39	387	512
--		32	178	385
5	331	50	546	420
3	716	38	897	871
6	329	87	659	782

85 percent of all direct foreign investment and 93 percent of all investments by U.S. companies.

[b]There are some differences in industrial classification in totals shown for companies and the published totals of the 1950 census. Census totals were derived by classifying each foreign organization of a United States parent company separately ac-

Table 4.3 Distribution of Foreign Investments by Industry and
Size Categories, 1950 (millions of dollars) (continued)

cording to the major activity of the unit. The companies data
were classified on the basis of all foreign operations of the
parent company together.

c Includes one company with foreign investments of more than
$25 million.

d Includes seven companies with investments of over $51 mil-
lion, accounting for a total foreign investment of $3.124 billion.

e Includes eleven companies with investments of over $51 mil-
lion, accounting for a total foreign investment of $1.373 billion.
Source: U.S. Department of Commerce, Factors Limiting U.S.
Investments Abroad, Part 2, Business Views on the U.S. Government's Role (Washington: U.S. Government Printing Office,
1954), pp. 48, 54.

Primary and Fabricated Metals Only one firm in pri-
once was; and the oligopolistic struggle surrounding
its foreign operations was noted earlier. Corn Products
Refining and the Coca-Cola Company are in the more
concentrated segments of the food industry; Heinz is
not.

Paper The four large investors in the paper industry
are the International Paper Company, with well over
$50 million invested in Canada, and three of the follow-
ing four, the Crown Zellerbach Corporation, the Kim-
berly-Clark Corporation, the Marathon Corporation,
and the Minnesota and Ontario Paper Company. This

industry is unlike other manufacturing industries, since the foreign investments are largely confined to Canada;[3] this is probably due to natural resources location.

Chemicals Two of the four chemical companies with foreign investments over $25 million in 1950 are two soap companies, the Procter and Gamble Company and the Colgate-Palmolive-Peet Company. It is not possible to tell which are the other two since the large chemical firms which might have substantial foreign investments, such as duPont, Union Carbide, or Allied Chemical and Dye, do not report their foreign activities in usable form. Sterling Drug, Incorporated, also has close to $25 million invested abroad and may be one of the large four. This illustrates the importance of pharmaceutical preparations. At least four other drug companies, Abbott Laboratories, American Home Products Corporation, Parke, Davis and Company, and E. R. Squibb and Sons, have foreign investments of more than $10 million. The drug industry, unlike the soap industry, is not concentrated as a whole but in individual products may be quite monopolistic.

[3]See Table 4.4.

Table 4.4 Value of United States Direct Investments in
Manufacturing[a] and Petroleum Enterprises Abroad, 1950, by
Major Products (millions of dollars)

	All Areas Total	Canada	Latin American Republics	United Kingdom	Other Western Europe	Other Areas
Petroleum	3,390	418	1,408	123	301	1,140
All manu- facturing[a]	3,831	1,897	780	542	390	222
Food products	483	227	158	36	28	34
Paper and allied products	378	367	5	1	4	1
Chemicals and allied products	512	198	205	54	21	34
Rubber products	182	59	60	21	10	32
Primary and fabricated metals	385	249	22	66	44	4
Machinery except electrical	420	204	13	108	67	28
Electrical machinery, equipment, and supplies	387	141	79	79	74	14
Motor vehi- cles and equipment	485	160	83	103	88	51
All other manufac- turing	599	292	155	74	54	24

Table 4.4 Value of United States Direct Investments in Manufacturing[a] and Petroleum Enterprises Abroad, 1950, by Major Products (millions of dollars) (continued)

---

[a]Excludes manufacturing operations of petroleum and mining companies.
Sources: 1. S. Pizer and F. Cutler, "Growth of Foreign Investments in the United States and Abroad," Survey of Current Business, XXXVI (August 1956), p. 22.
2. U.S. Department of Commerce, Office of Business Economics, Direct Private Foreign Investments of the United States, Census of 1950, p. 44.

mary and fabricated metals had over $25 million of assets, but it is not certain whether it is the American Radiator and Standard Sanitary Corporation or whether it is the American Can Company; both have close to $25 million of foreign investment. The Crane Company also has close to $25 million, and the Continental Can Company, Incorporated, has over $10 million. The Gillette Safety Razor Company (Delaware) has over $5 million, and the only primary metals company with substantial investment seems to be the Armco Steel Corporation. This accounts for six out of the seven firms with investment of from $6 to $25 million, although the coverage of this industry by the Office of Business Economics sample is not complete, as is seen in Table 4.3.[4]

<u>Machinery</u> Of the five large machinery companies
with more than $25 million of foreign investment, two
of them, the International Harvester Company and the
Singer Manufacturing Company, have more than $50
million, if not more than $100 million. The other three
firms are probably the International Business Machines
Corporation, United Shoe Machinery Corporation, and
the National Cash Register Company.

The eleven companies with foreign assets of from $6
to $25 million may be the following: the Allis-Chalmers
Manufacturing Company, the Bucyrus-Erie Company,
the Burroughs Adding Machine Company, the J. I. Case
Company, Deere and Company, the Hoover Company
(Ohio), Mergenthaler Linotype Company, the National
Supply Company, the Oliver Corporation, the Otis El-
evator Company (New Jersey), and Remington Rand,
Incorporated.

The office machinery and farm machinery industries
are obviously well represented.

The three large investors in the automotive and elec-

[4]It will be recalled (Table 4.1, footnote c) that manufacturing operations of mining and smelting companies
are not included in this category.

trical industry are the General Motors Corporation, the Ford Motor Company, and the General Electric Company. The first two of these have more than $50 million invested abroad. The other large automobile firms and electrical equipment firms also have important and often substantial foreign investments.

Other Industries The six large investors in the "other industries" category are the Eastman Kodak Company (with more than $50 million), Goodyear Tire and Rubber Company, Firestone Tire and Rubber Company, United States Rubber Company (at least two of these rubber companies had more than $50 million in assets), Lone Star Cement Corporation, and the Celanese Corporation of America.

Concentration The industries in which foreign investments are important are concentrated ones. Certainly this is true for automobiles, electrical equipment, rubber, business machinery and office machinery, shoe machinery, sewing machines, photographic equipment, elevators, corn products, soft drinks, soap, and razor blades, all of which have important foreign investments. These are compared to the industries where foreign investment is noticeably absent, natural fiber textiles, apparel, lumber, furniture, printing, leather, and so

forth. There are exceptions, of course. One striking
exception is the tobacco industry. But the story told
in Chapter 3 suggests that this may be because of the
existence of a strong foreign competitor in the Imperial
Tobacco Company. In any case, the association with
concentrated industries is not a simple one, and the
statement made earlier must be interpreted cautiously.

Size of Investing Firms The firms which do the investing are also large firms. The only statistical evidence
of this, aside from the fact that firms listed previously
are big firms, comes from Statistics of Income data.
In 1954, United States firms filing statements in support of their claims for foreign tax credit reported
$1.5 million of foreign income from all sources. Of
this $1.1 million applied to firms with $250 million of
assets or more.[5] To a limited extent, the large size
of investing firms supports the contention that they
dominate the industries they are in. Their size also
indicates that they are firms with a successful past and

[5]U.S. Treasury Department, Internal Revenue Service,
Statistics of Income for 1954, Corporation Income Tax
Returns (Washington: U.S. Government Printing Office,
1957), p. 130.

are likely to be firms with advantages (one of them may even be their size) in particular activities; these advantages are exploited abroad.

Cross Investment One of the most interesting aspects of international operations is that in many of the industries where American firms have substantial foreign operations, one of the firms operating in the United States is a foreign firm.

Industry	Foreign-Controlled Firms in the United States
1. Oil	Shell Oil Corporation
2. Soft drinks	Orange Crush, Ltd.
3. Paper	Bowater Paper Company
4. Soaps	Lever Brothers
5. Farm machinery	Massey-Harris-Ferguson Company
6. Business machinery	Moore Business Forms, Olivetti
7. Tires and tubes	Dunlop Tire and Rubber
8. Sewing machines	Necchi Sewing Machine Co.
9. Concentrated milk	Nestlé's
10. Biscuits	Weston's

This is not a complete list of foreign firms operating in the United States. It is restricted to those industries where American firms have foreign investments. The first eight of these cases are the very industries mentioned above where American international operations predominate. Except for paper and oil, they are all very concentrated industries. The last two (concen-

trated milk and biscuits) were not listed but are also

concentrated and have foreign investments. In concen-

trated milk, Dunning points out that the three firms

which supply most of the output in England are Libby,

McNeill, Libby, Ltd., Carnation Milk, Ltd., and

Nestlé's. The last two of these three also are impor-

tant producers of concentrated milk in the United

States.[6] In the biscuit industry, the National Biscuit

Company has extensive foreign operations.

The existence of cross investments is, it seems to

me, impressive and not at all contradictory to the the-

ory of international operations outlined earlier. But it

would be difficult to explain it by a theory of portfolio

investment which depends on interest rates or on pro-

fit rates in general instead of profit rates in particular,

that is, profitability to a particular firm. It appears

well worth further study. It occurs often enough to be

important yet not often enough to be a general rule.

[6]U.S. Federal Trade Commission, Report of the Federal Trade Commission on Industrial Concentration
and Product Diversification in the 1,000 Largest Manufacturing Companies: 1950 (Washington: U.S. Government Printing Office, 1957), p. 153.

One would like to know if it is possible to specify the
industry conditions which lead to cross investment. In
this connection it is interesting to watch the automobile
industry. The leading American companies have worldwide operations. Some of the foreign firms already
have investments in the United States in distribution
facilities; in the future, they may have manufacturing
operations as well.

The unevenness in the distribution of foreign investments which we tried to demonstrate really proves very
little. It was supposed to illustrate that certain industries have conditions favorable to international operations while other industries do not. But it actually did
not show this. For American firms could control a
constant percentage of all foreign industries; and yet
the distribution of foreign assets would differ from the
distribution of domestic assets, if the industrial composition of output was different abroad than it was at
home. What needs to be shown is that the American
share of foreign enterprise is consistently higher for
some industries than for others. To do this, we must
turn to data on American participation in specific countries. The distribution by countries of Unites States
direct investment in manufacturing is shown in Table 4.4.

We shall discuss, in turn, Canada, the United Kingdom,
Western Europe, and Latin America. For other countries there is no usable information readily available.

Canada

Industrial Distribution Table 4.5 shows the value added
in Canadian industries by all establishments and by selected United States-controlled establishments. The selected United States establishments are those of enterprises controlled in the United States and with assets
of more than $1 million in 1953. They account for 91
percent of the total United States investment in Canada.

The industries are ranked in descending order of American participation. It is interesting that the first seven
industries where Americans control 50 percent or more
of the industry account for $1.1 billion value added, or
almost half of the total value added by American-controlled enterprises. These industries are motor vehicles, nonferrous metal smelting and refining (aluminum, nickel, and so forth), rubber products, office
machinery, motor vehicle parts, petroleum products,
and electrical apparatus and supply. At the bottom of
the list are textiles, other iron and steel products,
beverages, bakery products and confectionery, primary

iron and steel, wood products, clothing, printing, publishing, and allied industries. This pattern is very similar to the one we discussed previously and have shown
in Tables 4.1 and 4.2, even though now the industries
are ranked by share of Canadian industry rather than
by the ratio to United States industry. The pattern would
be even more striking if some industries like shoe machinery, razor blades, sewing machines, elevators,
and so forth, were not so concentrated that they could
not be shown separately because of disclosure problems.

This pattern is repeated in other parts of the world.
Two important exceptions to the world pattern found in
Canada might be noted. There is substantial United
States investment in the paper industry in Canada but
not in the rest of the world. This is probably due to international trade considerations, for the United States
imports much pulp and paper from Canada and little
from other countries. As we mentioned in the last chapter, international operations are often determined by
the pattern of trade. It is the trade which brings about
the interdependence and creates the necessity for international operations. The other exception is in agricultural implements, where the United States share is

Table 4.5 Value Added in Canada for All Canadian Manufacturing Establishments and Value Added of Selected United
States-Controlled Establishments,[a] 1953 (millions of dollars)

Industry	Values Added by All Canadian Establish- ments	Value Added by Selected United States-Con- trolled Es- tablishments	Share of U.S.-Con- trolled Es- tablishments in Total Value Added Percent
Motor vehicles	274	266	97
Nonferrous metal smelting and refining	310	259	84
Rubber products	173	138	80
Machinery, household, office, and store	53	33	61
Motor vehicle parts	141	87	61
Petroleum products	160	93	59
Electrical apparatus and supplies	457	231	50
Soaps, washing com- pounds, and cleansing preparations	50	24	49
Paints, varnishes, and lacquers	57	26	46
Other nonferrous metal products	88	40	46
Other chemicals and allied products	260	108	41
Grain mill products	90	36	41
Medicinal and pharma- ceutical preparations	62	24	38
Pulp and paper	600	219	37
Brass and copper products	60	19	32
Machinery, industrial and machine tools	157	49	31
Sheet metal products	104	33	31

Table 4.5 Value Added in Canada for All Canadian Manufacturing Establishments and Value Added of Selected United States-Controlled Establishments,[a] 1953 (millions of dollars) (continued)

Industry	Values Added by All Canadian Establishments	Value Added by Selected United States-Controlled Establishments	Share of U.S.-Controlled Establishments in Total Value Added Percent
Heating and cooking apparatus	52	16	30
Canning and processing	132	38	28
Other paper products	167	46	28
Toilet preparations	19	5	26
Hardware, tools, and cutlery	85	20	23
Miscellaneous manufactures	155	34	22
Agricultural implements	79	17	21
Castings, iron	85	16	19
Aircraft and parts, railway rolling stock, and other transportation equipment	547	98	18
Nonmetallic mineral products and other products of petroleum and coal	292	49	17
Dairy products	121	21	17
Other food industries, tobacco and tobacco products, and leather products	459	69	15
Textile products except clothing	299	42	14
Other iron and steel products	308	43	14

Table 4.5 Value Added in Canada for All Canadian Manufacturing Establishments and Value Added of Selected United
States-Controlled Establishments,[a] 1953 (millions of dollars)
(continued)

Industry	Values Added by All Canadian Establishments	Value Added by Selected United States-Controlled Establishments	Share of U.S.-Controlled Establishments in Total Value Added Percent
Beverages	299	35	12
Bakery products and confections	224	25	11
Primary iron and steel	217	16	7
Wood products	577	30	5
Clothing (textiles and furs)	415	12	3
Printing, publishing, and allied	364	3	1
Total[b]	7,993	2,319	29

[a]Selected United States-controlled establishments refers to all
manufacturing establishments of United States-controlled enterprises with an aggregate investment in Canada of $1 million
or more. The 309 manufacturing enterprises falling within
this category covered 91 percent of the total investment of all
United States-controlled enterprises.

[b]Totals may not add exactly because of rounding.
Source: Dominion Bureau of Statistics, Canada's International
Investment Position 1926-1954 (Ottawa: Queen's Printer and
Controller of Stationery, 1958), p. 43, pp. 92-93.

only 21 percent, a figure which is lower than the one
found in other countries. This is, no doubt, influenced
by the fact that Canada is the home country of the Mas-
sey-Harris Company (now Massey-Harris-Ferguson),
one of the world's leading manufacturers of agricultural
equipment.

Table 4.6 shows data similar to those of Table 4.5,
but for the year 1932. The pattern is basically the
same.

Concentration The association of international operations with concentrated industries in Canada was noted
by Brecher and Reisman.

It is widely known that in many Canadian industries
a small number of large firms account for a high proportion of output; and that many of these companies are
owned and controlled by non-residents. In almost every
sector of Canadian industry where there is a significant
degree of non-resident investment, the average size of
enterprises controlled outside Canada is considerably
larger than their Canadian counterparts.[7]

Table 4.7 summarizes some evidence they present

[7]I. Brecher and S. S. Reisman, Canada-United States
Economic Relations (Ottawa: Queen's Printer and Controller of Stationery 1957), p. 278. This quotation and
the empirical evidence which follows are taken from
Appendix B of this book.

Table 4.6 Share of American-Controlled and American-Affiliated Companies in Gross Value of Product in Canada, 1932

Industry	American-Controlled or American-Affiliated Companies	
	Percent of Total Canadian Gross Value of Product Supplied (percent)	Capital Employed (millions of dollars)
Automobiles and trucking; automobile parts and accessories	82	51.9
Electrical apparatus	68	57.2
Rubber products	65	44.1
Medicinal and pharmaceutical preparations; soaps, washing components; toilet preparations	56	20.8
Nonferrous metals not elsewhere specified—including aluminum, brass, copper, lead, tin, zinc, and their products, precious metals, jewelry, and dental work	50	26.6
Nonmetallic minerals, including asbestos and its products, graphite and carbon, petroleum products, building materials	44	75.5
Agricultural implements, industrial machinery, office and household machinery	42	37.0
Miscellaneous manufactures— including brooms and brushes, household equipment, personal equipment, scientific and professional equipment	41	16.6
Pulp, paper, and lumber	34	266.0

Table 4.6 Share of American-Controlled and American-Affiliated Companies in Gross Value of Product in Canada, 1932 (continued)

Industry	American-Controlled or American-Affiliated Companies	
	Percent of Total Canadian Gross Value of Product Supplied (percent)	Capital Employed (millions of dollars)
Chemicals and allied products not elsewhere specified—including coal tar and its products; industrial chemicals and gas; fertilizers; paints, pigments and varnishes, inks, dyes, and colors	31	33.8
Iron and its products not elsewhere specified—including boilers, tanks and engines; railway rolling stock; heating and ventilating; wire and wire goods; sheet metal products; hardware and tools	25	53.8
Flour and cereals; prepared grain foods and confectionary	15	29.2
Furnaces and rolling mills; castings and forgings	12	32.6
Vegetable products not elsewhere specified—including fruit and vegetable preparations; liquors and cerated waters, sugar and its products	11	18.7
Animal products—including fish curing and packings; leather and leather products; wood products; dairy products	11	21.0

Table 4.6 Share of American-Controlled and American-Affiliated Companies in Gross Value of Product in Canada, 1932
(continued)

Industry	American-Controlled or American-Affiliated Companies	
	Percent of Total Canadian Gross Value of Product Supplied (percent)	Capital Employed (millions of dollars)
Wood and paper products not elsewhere specified—including paper goods; printing, publishing, and lithography; furniture, wooden containers; woodworking and turning	8	21.6
Textiles—including preparations of textile fibers; silk and silk goods; hosiery and knit garments and personal furnishings; embroidery, and lace work	8	26.9
All manufacturing	24	833.3

Source: H. Marshall, F. A. Southard, Jr., and K. W. Taylor,
Canadian-American Industry (New Haven: Yale University
Press, 1936), Table V, facing p. 24.

on concentration and nonresident control in Canada.
For each of selected industries, the table shows the
total value added by all establishments, the share of
value added accounted for by the six largest firms,
and the nationality of the six largest firms. Unfortunately, data are available for only a few industries,
and it is not possible to draw any general conclusions.
But of the seven industries shown in Table 4.5, where
United States-controlled establishments account for
50 percent or more of the value added in Canadian industry, data on concentration are available for all but
one. The data in Table 4.7 do cover motor vehicles,
nonferrous metal smelting and refining, rubber products, motor vehicle parts, petroleum products, and
electrical apparatus and supplies. All are concentrated
industries. The industry for which concentration data
are not available is the household, office, and store
machinery industry. Its concentration is not known. It
is also interesting to observe that in the twenty industries listed in Table 4.7, a United States-controlled
firm was the largest firm in thirteen industries and
the second-largest in thirteen industries.[8]

[8]Ibid., pp. 278-285.

Table 4.7 Concentration Ratios and Nationality of Six Leading
Firms for Selected Canadian Industries, 1953

Industry	Value Added by All Firms ($ mill)	Value Added of Six Largest Firms as a Percent of Total Value Added (percent)	Nationality of Six Largest Firms			
			Canadian	U.S.	Other	Total
Petroleum						
Crude petroleum	241	68	1	5	0	6
Petroleum refining	301	93	1	4	1	6
Mining smelting and refining						
Nickel-copper	244	100	3	3	0	6
Lead-zinc	89	86	4	1	1	6
Copper-gold	114	86	4	2	0	6
Iron ore	35	100	3	3	0	6
Aluminum[a]	—	—	0	1	0	1
Asbestos	72	94	3	2	1	6
Gypsum	5	97	2	3	1	6
Manufacturing						
Pulp and paper	641	46	4	1	1	6
Chemicals						
Fertilizers[b]	40	92	2	2	1	5
Acids, alkalies, and salts	79	63	1	3	2	6
Elec. app. supplies	463	52	2	4	0	6
Primary iron and steel	217	84	5	1	0	6

Table 4.7 Concentration Ratios and Nationality of Six Leading
Firms for Selected Canadian Industries, 1953 (continued)

Industry	Value Added by All Firms ($ mill)	Value Added of Six Largest Firms as a Percent of Total Value Added (percent)	Nationality of Six Largest Firms			
			Canadian	U.S.	Other	Total
Automobiles	176	97	0	6	0	6
Rubber goods	149	77	1	5	0	6
Railway rolling stock	117	84	2	3	1	6
Primary textiles Synthetic fibers[c]	47	100	0	3	1	4
Exc. synthetic	70	90	6	0	0	6
Agricultural implements[d]	49	91	2	2	0	4

[a]Only one firm in this industry.

[b]Data on nationality available for only five of the six firms.

[c]Four largest producers only.

[d]Data on nationality available for only four of the six firms.
Source: I. Brecher and S. S. Reisman, Canada-United States
Economic Relations, (Ottawa: Queen's Printer and Controller
of Stationery, 1957), Appendix B, pp. 278-285.

Size of Foreign-Controlled Firms One of the striking
features about the Canadian data is the high percentage
of large firms which are controlled by non-Canadians.
Of the eighty-two firms in Canada with over $25 mil-
lion of assets in 1953 in the petroleum, mining, and
manufacturing industries, more than half were controlled by non-Canadians. The industrial distribution
and the nationality of firms in Canada with assets of
more than $25 million in 1953 is shown in Table 4.8.

United Kingdom
For the United Kingdom there is the excellent study of
American international operations by John H. Dunning,[9]
upon which the following discussion is based. This
study covers 245 firms which Dunning believes to be
all the firms in the United Kingdom in which Americans had a 25 percent or greater equity capital interest and which employed more than 100 workers in
December 1953. Only 205 of these firms cooperated
with Dunning, and it is on the reports of these 205
firms that his data are based. Dunning believes that

[9]John H. Dunning, American Investment in British
Manufacturing Industry (London: George Allen and
Unwin Ltd., 1958).

Table 4.8 Nationality of Firms Operating in Selected Canadian
Industries in 1953 with Assets of $25 Million or More

	Number of Firms in Canada with Assets of $25 Million or More in 1953 in Selected Industries			
	All Nation-alities	Canadian-Controlled	U.S.-Controlled	Controlled in Other Countries
Total	82	38	38	6
Petroleum	13	2	9	2
Mining	14	7	7	0
Manufacturing	55	29	22	4
Pulp and paper			6	
Chemicals			4	
Electrical apparatus and supplies			2	
Automobiles and parts			4	
Rubber goods			2	
Agricultural machinery			1	
Aluminum			1	
Synthetic textiles			1	
Meat products			1	

Source: Brecher and Reisman, Canada-United States Economic
Relations, Appendix B, pp. 285-287.

these firms employ between 90 percent and 95 percent
of the total labor force of United States financial manufacturing units in the United Kingdom.[10]

Industrial Distribution The industrial distribution of
the American firms is presented in Table 4.9, where
the industries are arranged in descending order of
American participation. Again we find chemicals, vehicles, engineering and shipbuilding (which includes
office and agricultural machinery), and electrical goods
at the top of the list, while textiles and clothing are at
the bottom. This table greatly underestimates the unevenness of the distribution of American investment because the industrial categories are so broad. To demonstrate this, we shall quote extensively from Dunning's
text in which he constantly refers to the concentration
in particular industries.

These quotations will show the specialized nature of
United States international operations in the United
Kingdom. Unfortunately, data on the American share
of United Kingdom industries are presented by Dunning
for only a few of the subindustries. These estimates,

[10]Ibid., p. 12.

Table 4.9 Numbers Employed by All Firms and by United
States Firms Operating in the United Kingdom, 1953

	U.S. Firms No.	Employment	U.S. Firms Employment	All Firms Employment	U.S. Firms Share of Total Employment (percent)
Precision instruments	9	16,200		138,300	11.7
Chemicals and allied trades	48	31,300		498,800	6.3
Vehicles	6	56,000		1,121,900	5.0
Engineering and shipbuilding	67	77,000		1,604,000	4.8
Electrical goods	10	13,600		329,200	4.1
Food, drink, tobacco	13	16,400		844,100	1.9
Metal manufactures	11	8,400		551,100	1.5
Wood, cork, paper and printing manufactures	7	4,400		300,400	1.5
Other manufactures	25	16,500		1,212,310	1.4
Metal goods—not otherwise specified	2	2,500		491,300	.5
Textiles and clothing	7	3,900		1,640,000	.2
	205	246,200		8,732,000	2.8

Source: J. H. Dunning, American Investment in British Manufacturing Industry (London: George Allen and Unwin Ltd.,
1958), p. 58.

though not complete in their coverage, provide support
to the propositions we have been trying to establish in
this chapter. The estimates of market shares are
shown in Table 4.10, which should be referred to in
conjunction with the discussion to follow. This table
is meant to be illustrative. The omission of an industry does not imply that the American share is low but
just that data are not available. For example, some
cases were omitted where Dunning states that the American firm was the largest or a prominent producer but
where he did not provide data on shares.

Chemicals and Allied Trades Dunning says of this industry:

> Of the forty-eight American firms included within
> our survey, forty were highly specialized in their pro-
> duction and were all concentrated within five main sec-
> tors of the industry, viz:—basic chemicals, mineral
> oil refining, pharmaceutical preparations, cosmetics
> and toilet articles and soap products. How selective
> U.S. investment has been is shown by the fact that
> these groups between them employ less than one-half
> the total labour force in the chemical industry.[11]

Even this underestimates specialization. For example, within the basic chemicals industry, Dunning
states:

[11]Ibid., pp. 59-60.

Only one Anglo-American company—the Monsanto
Chemical Co., Ltd. (assets £14.4 million)—might be
called an all-purpose chemical supplier, with its production of over 200 basic materials which serve a
wide range of industries; and this is one of the three
largest manufacturers of its kind in this country.
Otherwise investment in this field has been limited
to the production of certain specialized materials.[12]

Vehicles Dunning found that in this industry,

American participation is solely confined to the manufacturing of motor vehicles and motor vehicle acces-
sories and components. As far as we know, no firms
of American origin are producing aircraft (though a
number of subsidiaries are supplying specialized aircraft components); neither is any capital evident in the
bicycle or motorcycle industries.[13]

Engineering and Shipbuilding Dunning states that

Once again, however, investment tends to be confined to a relatively small number of selective fields.
There is, for example, little or no U.S. capital at
present invested in the shipbuilding and ship repairing,
marine engineering, ordnance constructional engineering, electrical machinery and small arms, wireless
valves and electric lamps and battery and accumulator
sections of the industry, which between them account
for 35 percent of the total labour force of the group as
a whole.[14]

[12]Ibid., p. 60.

[13]Ibid., p. 71.

[14]Ibid., p. 65.

Table 4.10 Share of United States Firms in Selected United
Kingdom Industries

Industry	Estimated Share of United States Firms in United Kingdom Industry (Dunning's terminology)
Chemicals and allied trades	
Carbon black	Three-quarters
Phenol plastics	Substantial
Petroleum refining	One-third
Pharmaceutical products, antibiotics	One-fifth to one-half All
Toilet preparations and cosmetics	One-half
Vehicles	
Motor vehicles	Two-fifths
Engineering and shipbuilding	
Agricultural machinery[a]	60 to 70 percent
Calculating machines and cash registers	One-half to two-thirds
Typewriters	One-half
Shoe machinery	Almost all
Sewing machinery	Almost all
Refrigerators	One-third to one-half
Electric switches	Two-thirds
Food, drink, and tobacco	
Starch	Practically all
Custards	Largely

Table 4.10 Share of United States Firms in Selected United
Kingdom Industries (continued)

Industry	Estimated Share of United States Firms in United Kingdom Industry (Dunning's terminology)
Evaporated milk[b]	Greater part
Processed cheese	Three-quarters
Breakfast cereals	All
Chewing gum	Most of
Metal manufactures and metal goods not otherwise specified	
Domestic boilers	60 percent
Nickel	100 percent
Razor blades	90 percent
Cigarette lighters[c]	100 percent
Textiles and clothing	
Foundation garments	Two-thirds
Other manufacturing industries	
Talking picture apparatus	40 percent
Vehicle tires	Two-fifths
Cinematic films	90 percent
Roll films	Two-fifths
Abrasives	40 percent

[a]Two American firms and one Anglo-Canadian firm—Massey-
Harris-Ferguson.

Table 4.10   Share of United States Firms in Selected United
Kingdom Industries (continued)

---

[b]Two American firms and one Swiss firm—Nestlé's.

[c]Market share refers to years before 1946 when the Ronson
patent expired.
Source: Dunning, American Investment in British Manufacturing Industry, pp. 60-78.

Of the 77,000 employees in American firms in the
engineering and shipbuilding industries, 27,000 were
employed in two of the subindustries, agricultural
equipment (16,000) and office machinery (11,000). Petroleum field and refining equipment was also an important sector, as well as a number of more specialized sections: lifts and escalators, shoe machinery,
printing and typesetting machinery, refrigeration machinery, materials handling equipment, specialized
mining equipment, food production machinery, petrol
pumps, air-conditioning equipment, laundry machinery,
road-making equipment, bottle-washing machinery,
catering and dairy equipment.[15] Dunning concludes
that "where there is any American representation in

[15]Ibid., pp. 64-70.

the engineering industry, it is an important one."[16]

<u>Food, Drink and Tobacco</u> Dunning comments that

Comprising a wide range of separate trades, this
industry employed nearly one million people in December 1954. U.S. influence is once more restricted to a
number of selected fields.[17]

Among these selected fields are starch, custards,

evaporated milk, processed cheese, breakfast cereals,

and ready-made cake mixes.

<u>Metal Manufacturing and Metal Goods Not Otherwise</u>

<u>Specified</u> Dunning says that

There are no American firms in the blast furnace
and wrought-iron sections, and whilst in steel manufacturing a number of important British companies ...
enjoy an exchange of technical know-how with U.S.
firms, the influence of American capital is small.[18]

American firms have investments in the boiler in-

dustry and in the manufacture of heating appliances.

Apart from this, "U.S. influence is restricted to a

number of specialist fields."[19]

<u>Textiles and Clothing</u> American participation is al-

---

[16]Ibid., p. 71.

[17]Ibid., p. 75.

[18]Ibid., p. 74.

[19]Ibid., p. 75.

most entirely concentrated in the foundation garment,

swim wear, and lingerie section.[20]

Other Manufacturing Industries   For our last example

to illustrate the concentration of American industry,

it is sufficient to point out that of the 16,500 employees

listed in the category "other manufacturing industries"

in Table 4.9, 11,000 were in one subindustry, namely

the rubber industry.[21]

Concentration   The connection between concentrated

industries and international operations is nowhere

more clearly seen than in the data presented by Dun-

ning. He states (without supporting evidence) that

"three-quarters of the employment in U.S. affiliated

firms is concentrated in industries where the five

largest competitors supply 80 percent or more of total

output."[22] He also presents a very revealing table

shown here as Table 4.11. This table also serves to

illustrate further the specialized nature of international

operations. The table shows that of the 246,000 em-

ployees of American-controlled firms, 32,000 are em-

[20]Ibid., p. 72.

[21]Ibid., p. 77.

[22]Ibid., p. 155.

ployed in industries where the American firm is a dominant producer, and 200,000 others are employed by
firms in an industry where the American firm is one
of a small number of strong producers. The predominance of oligopolistic industries is striking. The table
also indicates that the American firms are large firms
relative to other firms in the same industry.

Western Europe

For the rest of the world, the data are even poorer than
those for Canada and for the United Kingdom. The main
source of information on Europe other than the United
Kingdom is a study made by Southard in 1931.[23] It is
old and not very complete but still illuminating. Perhaps its age is not too much of a disadvantage, for it
may serve to illustrate that the phenomena we have been
discussing are not merely products of recent years. On
the other hand, the many changes which have occurred
in Europe (especially in recent years in response to the
advent of the common market) stress the need for current research.

   One of the interesting features about the international

[23] F. A. Southard, Jr., American Industry in Europe
(Cambridge, Mass.: The Riverside Press, 1931), p. xiii.

Table 4.11 Importance of United States-Financed Firms in British Industry

Group A U.S. Firm the Dominant Producer	Group B[a] U.S. Firm One of a Small Number of Strong Producers	Group C U.S. Firm One of a Number of Producers of Modest Size
12 firms employing 32,000 people	136 firms employing 200,000 people	57 firms employing 14,000 people
Products supplied:	Within such an industrial structure U.S.-financed firms are the largest producers of:	Products supplied:
Sewing machines	Domestic boilers	Proprietary medicines
Boot and shoe machinery	Breakfast cereals	Beauty and toilet preparations
Starch	Synthetic detergents	Industrial instruments
Carbon black	Foundation garments	Petroleum refinery equipment
Cinematic films*	Printing and type-setting machinery	Machine and hand tools
Motor vehicle tire valves	Oil drilling equipment	Cigarettes
	Road-making machinery	Foundation garments
	Sparking plugs	Cotton textiles
	Roll films	
	Lifts and escalators	
	Safety razors and blades	

Table 4.11 Importance of United States-Financed Firms in
British Industry (continued)

Group A U.S. Firm the Dominant Producer	Group B[a] U.S. Firm One of a Small Number of Strong Producers	Group C U.S. Firm One of a Number of Producers of Modest Size
12 firms employing 32,000 people	136 firms employing 200,000 people	57 firms employing 14,000 people
	Typewriters	
	Cash registers	
	Calculating machines	
	Refined platinum	
	Commercial refrigerators	
	Vacuum cleaners	
	the second largest producers of:	
	Motorcars	
	Agricultural tractors and implements	
	Rubber tires	
	Abrasives and grinding wheels	
	Canned milk	
	Canned foodstuffs	
	Soft drinks	
	Home refrigerators	

Table 4.11 Importance of United States-Financed Firms in
British Industry (continued)

Group A U.S. Firm the Dominant Producer	Group B[a] U.S. Firm One of a Small Number of Strong Producers	Group C U.S. Firm One of a Number of Producers of Modest Size
12 firms employing 32,000 people	136 firms employing 200,000 people	57 firms employing 14,000 people
	Electronic indus- trial instruments	
	Alarm clocks	
	Portable electric tools	
	Excavating equipment	
	and the third largest producers of:	
	All-purpose chemicals	
	Rubber tires	
	Refined petroleum	
	Hardboard	

*Subject to foreign competition.

[a]Also included in Group B are firms supplying ethical drug spe-
cialties, telephone equipment, pneumatic tools, petrol pumps,
bottle-washing machinery, cat and dog food, motion picture
sound-projection equipment, and electric washing machines.
Source: Dunning, American Investment in British Manufacturing Industry, pp. 156-157.

operations of the United States is the fact that the firms
which are now the large foreign investors began their
foreign operations so very long ago. In Chapter 1 we
mentioned the fact that in Great Britain, 115,200 employees out of the total 205,000 in Dunning's sample
worked for firms which were established before 1914.[24]
Something similar may be true for Europe as a whole.
Although we have no direct evidence, the following quotation from Southard is relevant:

> But it was the two decades just prior to the opening
> of the present century which saw a startling develop-
> ment, the export of capital in significant amounts by
> American corporations for the establishment of Eu-
> ropean plants and sales organizations, at a time when
> the United States was steadily importing capital. In
> this period the American meat packers, the Standard
> Oil Company, the Eastman Kodak Company, the Worth-
> ington Simpson Company, the American Radiator Com-
> pany, the Western Electric Company, the National Cash
> Register Company, the Singer Sewing Machine Com-
> pany, the General Electric Company—to name only a
> few—established plants in Europe which in almost every
> case are still actively operating.[25]

With the exception of the Worthington Simpson Company and the Western Electric Company, all the other

---

[24]Dunning, American Investment in British Manufacturing Industry, p. 95.

[25]Southard, American Industry in Europe, p. xiii.

firms were on the list of the twenty-seven manufacturing firms with investment of more than $25 million
discussed previously. Western Electric would have
been on that list were it not in public utilities and had
its foreign holdings not been taken over by International
Telephone and Telegraph Company.

Industrial Distribution Southard does discuss and de-
scribe the main industries in Europe where United
States-controlled enterprises are important. These
industries are electrical equipment, electric power,
telephone and telegraph (both equipment and supplies),
petroleum, automobiles, mines and metals, motion
pictures, drugs and chemicals, rubber tires, phono-
graphs, locks and keys.

We are interested mainly in illustrating the industrial specialization and the concentrated nature of the
industries where American firms have international
operations. We have selected, therefore, those quotations from Southard which throw light on these points;
that is, we selected all quotations on the market share
of United States firms in European industry. As will
be seen in many cases, the market shares are quite
high.

The Electrical Equipment Industry The bulk of United

States international operations in this industry is accounted for by two firms, the General Electric Company and the Westinghouse Electric Company. Southard's
summary of the extent of American penetration in this
industry is shown in the following quotation.

In England the American companies exert a dominant
influence over approximately 50 percent of the industry.
Only one large company, the General Electric Company,
Ltd., remains independent, and even it has a patent
agreement with the leading American company.

In Germany, American influence is dominant in one
of the two great companies, while the other is finan-
cially indebted to and has an agreement with American
corporations.

The French industry is almost completely under American influence and direction, with only one company of
importance, the Compagnie Générale Electricité, re-
taining independence save for a patent agreement.

The European incandescent lamp industry is completely linked up with the leading American producer
through patent agreements and stock ownership. Quantitative estimates of the importance of American interests in the rest of Europe are not possible, but it
may be stated that the leading companies are in almost
every case subject to American influence.[26]

Electric Power Industry Southard comments that

Only in England is a substantial portion of the industry under American control. In France and Italy American power finance corporations exert considerable in-

[26]Ibid., p. 36.

fluence through minority stock interests and financial
support, but the industry is, nominally at least, locally controlled.[27]

Telephone and Telegraph Equipment Industry The International Telephone and Telegraph Corporation was
in 1931 the largest of the American companies in
Europe and the largest of the European companies as
well. There seem to be three main groups in the telephone and telegraph industry in Europe, and of these
the American group was the largest.[28]

The Petroleum Industry With reference to petroleum
production in Europe, Southard states that at that time
(1931) it was "largely a story of the Standard Oil of
New Jersey competing with the Shell group in Roumania
and with the Malapolska combine (reported to be supported by Shell) in Poland."[29]

   In marketing of petroleum products, Southard estimates that the American companies supply one-third
of the market in France and about one-half of the market in Germany. No data are available for the rest of
Europe.[30]

[27]Ibid., pp. 41-42.
[28]Ibid., p. 55.
[29]Ibid., p. 60.
[30]Ibid., pp. 68-69.

Motor Vehicles Southard states that

The American motor-car producers in Europe are becoming increasingly important in comparison with the European producers. The total European output is approximately 600,000 cars per year, the bulk being confined to cars below 18 h.p., which is roughly the lower limit for American motor cars. The 110,000 American cars exported to Europe, coupled with the possible 40,000 others completely assembled there, constitute a large proportion of the cars over 18 h.p. sold in Europe.[31]

Mines and Metals Southard's comment follows:

A quantitative estimate of the importance of the American metal interests in Europe is not feasible with the data available. In Poland roughly 50 percent of the steel and an even larger proportion of the zinc, and 30 percent of the coal is under American control. In Norway the electric smelting industry, especially in aluminum, is largely American owned. The English nickel industry is now controlled from America, while the lead and tin industry feels American influence. The remaining American investments are scattered and have little relative importance.[32]

The Motion Picture Industry The talking-picture equipment was supplied by two groups, one of which is American. The motion picture market was, up to the advent of talking pictures, supplied largely by American firms. "In 1929, 75 percent of the English, 48 percent of the

[31]Ibid., p. 29.
[32]Ibid., p. 93.

French and 33 percent of the German market were
served with American films. In many of the smaller
European countries the American motion picture retained its position of dominance."[33]

The Drugs and Chemicals Industry In this industry,
there were a large number of American firms (twenty-
two), but they were small compared to I.G. Farben-
industrie.

The Rubber Industry Southard offers no estimate of
market shares in the rubber industry.

The Phonograph Industry Here the field is "divided
between three groups; two American and one, now
English, erstwhile American."[34]

The Lock and Keys Industry The last industry for which
Southard provides an estimate of market shares is the
lock and keys industry, where the American firm is the
largest producer of locks in Europe. Southard does list
other industries, but no estimate of market shares of
American firms is available, although in some industries, for example, sewing machines, it may very well
be quite high. But we really do not know.

[33]Ibid., p. 102.
[34]Ibid., p. 108.

Latin America

There is a 1934 study of American investments in
Argentina, Brazil, Uruguay, and Chile from which
Table 4.12 was obtained.[35] This study provides information on the industrial distribution of United States
investments but unfortunately gives no estimate of the
share of American firms in Latin American industry.
There is no other source from which an estimate of
the share can be obtained. But a crude method of illustrating the unevenness of the distribution is possible.
In a 1955 study the Department of Commerce published
figures on the industrial and national distribution of the
sales of American direct investments in Latin America.[36]
These data are presented in Table 4.13. From these data
it is possible to compute the percentage distribution of
sales of American subsidiaries by industry and to compare the distribution with the composition of industrial
output in selected Latin American countries as obtained

---

[35]D. M. Phelps, Migration of Industry to South America
(New York: McGraw-Hill Book Company, Inc., 1936).

[36]U.S. Department of Commerce, Office of Business
Economics, U.S. Investments in the Latin American
Economy (Washington: U.S. Government Printing Of-
fice, 1957), p. 132.

Table 4.12 United States Capital Invested in Selected
Industries in Argentina, Brazil, Uruguay, and Chile in 1934
(millions of dollars)

Industry	United States Capital Invested
Meat packing	94.6
Petroleum	55.1
Miscellaneous[a]	29.8
Automobiles and tires	26.5
Construction materials, including cement	21.4
Food (other than meat packing)	3.3
Phonographs and radios	2.1
Pharmaceutical	1.7
Total[b]	234.6

[a] In this group $25 million are accounted for by the following
seven firms: General Electric Company, Brazilian Traction,
Light and Power Co., Ltd., Pullman Standard Car Export
Corporation, E. I. duPont deNemours and Company, Consoli-
dated Chemical Industries, Inc., National Lead, W. R. Grace
and Co.

[b] Total may not add because of rounding.
Source: D. M. Phelps, Migration of Industry to South America
(New York: McGraw-Hill Book Company, Inc., 1936), p. 24.

from various sources. The procedure is crude, and
the results not very convincing, but for what they are
worth, the data for Brazil are presented in Table 4.14,
and for Argentina, Chile, Colombia, and Venezuela in
Table 4.15. For one industry at least, the rubber industry, the results are clear. Relative to its importance in total industrial output, it accounts for a high
share of international operations. For other industries,
at least the unevenness of the distribution can be observed.

Conclusions

We have surveyed a wide variety of material from several sources. As the reader can well appreciate, the
data are woefully inadequate. We were trying to illustrate that the pattern of international operations (or
direct investment) of the United States has certain
features consistent with the theory of previous chapters. These features are based on the theory that international operations occur in some industries throughout the world rather than in all industries in some countries. The rationale of this is that international operations are a phenomenon of firms and the industries, in
contrast to portfolio capital movements, which depend

Table 4.13 Sales by United States Manufacturing Companies
Operating in Latin America, 1955 (millions of dollars)

	Argentina	Brazil	Chile
Food	214	110	a
Chemicals and allied products	81	48	6
Rubber products	42	51	6
Metals and nonelectrical machinery	12	32	1
Electrical machinery	37	32	5
Motor vehicles and equipment	21	56	8
All other manufacturing	32	28	27
All industries[b]	438	357	53

[a]Less than $500,000.

[b]Data given cover only companies reported in special survey.
These companies account for 90 percent of the operations of
all companies in Latin America. Totals may not add up exactly
because of rounding.
Source: U.S. Department of Commerce, Office of Business
Economics, U.S. Investments in the Latin American Economy
(Washington: U.S. Government Printing Office 1957), p. 132.

Colombia	Cuba	Mexico	Venezuela	Other Countries	Latin America Total
8	33	22	13	17	416
25	27	129	13	14	342
5	9	23	6	7	149
3	0	23	6	1	77
a	0	34	0	5	113
0	0	70	46	14	214
28	14	16	10	40	196
69	83	316	93	98	1,507

Table 4.14 Industrial Distribution of Total Value of Manufactured Products in Brazil in 1956 and Industrial Distribution of Sales by United States Manufacturing Companies Operating in Brazil in 1955

Industry as Defined for		Percent Distribution of Sales by United States Companies	Percent Distribution of Total Value of Manufactured Products in Brazil
Sales of United States Firms	Total Value of Manufactured Products in Brazil		
Food	Food, beverages, and tobacco products	31	26
Chemicals and allied products	Chemicals and pharmaceuticals	13	14
Rubber products	Rubber and products	14	3
Metals and nonelectrical machinery	Metallurgy and machinery	9	13
Motor vehicles and equipment	Transportation equipment	16	3
Electrical machinery	Electrical equipment	9	4
All other manufacturing	All other manufacturing	8	37
Total		100	100

Table 4.14   Industrial Distribution of Total Value of Manufactured Products in Brazil in 1956 and Industrial Distribution of Sales by United States Manufacturing Companies Operating in Brazil in 1955 (continued)

Source: 1. Distribution of sales of United States companies is derived from data in Table 4.13.
2. Percent distribution of total value of manufactured products in Brazil, Stanford Research Institute, International Industrial Development Centre, International Comparative Studies, Investment Series I, Brazil—Factors Affecting Foreign Investment (Menlo Park, Calif.: Stanford Research Institute, 1958), p. 9.

on general conditions of a country, such as the interest rate.

The data we presented did show that international operations were concentrated in selected industries, and in a rough way it was shown that the industries in which international operations are important are the same in all countries. The tendency for these industries to be concentrated industries was also shown, and in the case of the United Kingdom it was particularly striking.

As we stated in the beginning of the chapter, empirical investigation of international operations is very difficult because it requires detailed studies of firms and industries on a worldwide basis. It is seldom possible

Table 4.15 Industrial Distribution of Total Value of Output of Manufactured Products in Argentina, Chile, Colombia, and Venezuela, and Industrial Distribution of Sales by United States Manufacturing Companies Operating in These Countries[a]

Industry as Defined for Sales of U.S. Companies	Value of Production for Economy	Argentina Percent Distribution of	
		Sales of U.S. Companies	Total Value of Production
Food	Foodstuffs and beverages	49	20
Chemicals and allied products	Chemical and pharmaceutical products	19	8
Rubber products	Rubber products	10	2
Metals, machinery (electrical and nonelectrical) and motor vehicles and equipment	Metals and their manufacture, machinery and vehicles	16	23
All other manufacturing	All other manufacturing	7	47
Total[c]		100	100

[a]Data on sales of United States companies are for 1955. Data for distribution of value of output are for 1955 for Argentina and Venezuela but for 1952 for Chile and 1953 for Colombia.

[b]Less than 1 percent.

[c]Totals may not add up to 100 percent because of rounding.
Source: 1. Sales of United States companies are derived from data in Table 4.13.
2. Distribution data of total value of product are from United Nations, Economic Commission for Latin America, Economic Survey of Latin America 1956 (New York: United Nations, 1957), p. 78.

Chile		Colombia		Venezuela	
Percent Distribution of		Percent Distribution of		Percent Distribution of	
Sales of U.S. Companies	Total Value of Production	Sales of U.S. Companies	Total Value of Production	Sales of U.S. Companies	Total Value of Production
b	30	12	42	15	44
11	8	36	7	15	2
11	2	7	4	7	3
26	16	4	6	52	0
51	44	41	41	10	51
100	100	100	100	100	100

to acquire information either in sufficient detail or with
worldwide coverage. For some industries—motor vehicles, tires and tubes, and petroleum products—enough
information is perhaps available to make a study possible.[37] But for other industries it is very difficult. The
author tried to get microdata by examining the annual
reports of 750 large American manufacturing firms.
The annual reports are informative but not sufficiently
so. As was evident earlier, it was not possible to determine exactly the investment of even the twenty-seven
firms with foreign investment of $25 million or more.
In the absence of more consistent reporting by firms,
it is not possible to acquire data from which to derive
general propositions subject to reasonably reliable statistical tests. Nor does the future hold much hope for
this source. Firms separate their foreign and domestic
activities in reporting mainly because of the feeling that
greater risk is attached to their foreign activities. This

[37]George Fishman, for his bachelor's thesis at M.I.T.,
is making a very interesting study of the world automobile industry and the roles of individual firms. Unfortunately, his thesis is not yet complete, and his results could not be quoted at this time. [For an up-to-
date study—post-1975—see the forthcoming book on the
European automobile industry by Louis T. Wells.—CPK]

tendency was accentuated by the international difficul-

ties of the past fifteen years. As conditions improved,

many firms reverted to a policy of consolidating for-

eign activities with domestic activities. (This is par-

ticularly evident for the case of Canada; relatively few

firms distinguish between "United States" and "Canada"

in their accounting data.) An interview program might

be possible were it not for the reluctance of firms to

release data. In any case, the Department of Com-

merce is probably the only body with adequate resources,

but it tends to collect data on an establishment basis,

whereas for international operations the firm is the

relevant unit. (Because of the concentrated nature of

industries with international operations, the disclosure

limitation on government data is particularly restric-

tive.)

Even if microdata were available, the problem of

estimating market shares would be a difficult one be-

cause data on industry output in foreign countries is

often nonexistent. This difficulty is, however, being

lessened with improvements in census material. The

Canadian information is quite good, and in the United

Kingdom, Dunning was able to make considerable head-

way. There probably will soon be much data on direct

investment in the common market. But for the rest of the world, especially Latin America, much work needs to be done. The work would, I think, be important. Studies of the structure of industries throughout the world (rather than, as in the past, within countries) would be most revealing because they would provide the economist with data on industries influenced by a wider variety of conditions than is true for industries within countries. However, as of now, these studies are rare.

This ends the discussion of the theory of international operations which has occupied us for three chapters. In the next chapter we discuss the manner in which capital is associated with international operations.

5

DIRECT INVESTMENT AND THE FINANCING OF
INTERNATIONAL OPERATIONS

Introduction

Chapter 1 argued that the interest-rate theory of capital movements, much as it might apply to portfolio
investment, was not in itself adequate to explain direct
investment. Instead, it was suggested that direct investment was capital associated with international operations and that to understand the movement of direct
investment, we had first to explain international operations. International operations, as it were, provided
the demand for direct investment. This point is important because the demand for capital for international
operations behaves differently from other demands for
capital. Direct investment, therefore, can and does
behave differently from portfolio.

We have discussed so far the causes of international
operations, but we have not discussed how international
operations lead to direct investment. In this chapter we
turn to this problem of the relation of capital movements
to international operations. In particular we try to explain the empirical phenomenon presented in Chapter 1:
namely, that the United States companies finance only
part (53 percent, to be exact) of the capital needs of
their international operations from the United States—
the rest is financed through local sources in the country

where the operations occur. Moreover, most of the
capital which comes from the United States is invested
in equity capital, which implies control, while most of
the capital borrowed in the foreign country is creditor
capital, which does not usually involve control.

In the discussion of the causes of international operations, capital played an important role in two quite opposite senses: first, as a cause of international operations; second, as a cause of not having international
operations. Capital was a cause of international operations because one of the advantages possessed by American firms over firms of other nationalities was cheaper
capital. This was especially true where large blocks of
capital were needed to finance large indivisible investments. On the other hand, an American firm might
have a disadvantage in acquiring capital, and this might
lead it to license instead of operating itself. When a
firm licenses, it is the foreigner who supplies the capital.

There is empirical evidence that both phenomena occur at the same time, that is, in some instances American firms have cheaper sources of capital and in other
instances, more expensive sources. This is not at all
strange. It occurs because there is no single interest

rate in a country; rather, there are many interest
rates; in fact, there may be one for each firm. This
feature of capital markets is extremely important, for
the relationship of direct investment to international
operations is determined largely by the imperfections
which lead to fractured capital markets.

There are two questions to be answered. First, how
does a particular firm decide how much to finance in
each country? Obviously, it borrows in the cheapest
market. But what is the cheapest market? This is a
complex question, and it is not simply a matter of
which country has the lowest interest rate. Second,
given a method of financing, that is, given a decision
of how much to borrow in each country, what impact
does this have on the world distribution of capital and
the world interest rate?

The importance and interest of both of these questions arise from imperfections in the capital market.
This is in contrast to portfolio investment, where the
pure theory really depends on a perfect market.

The Perfect Capital Market
Consider a really perfect capital market—perfect certainty, perfect information, and no transactions costs
or barriers to movement—where everyone can borrow

as much as he wants at the same interest rate. This
is the type of market generally used for theories of
the interest rate. For if the assumptions of perfection
are dropped, analysis becomes extremely difficult and
complex.

In such a market, given tastes, production possibilities, and initial distribution of wealth, the interest rate
is determined, and the volume of capital movements
between markets (in our particular case, between countries) is determined. This model is the basis for the
familiar treatment of international capital movements
into which some imperfections gradually are introduced.
It is a very fruitful approach.

What becomes of the two problems of international
operations in this model? The first problem of how
much the firm raises in each capital market becomes
meaningless. It is all one market, and the interest rate
is the same anywhere. But this is a trivial observation.

More significant, whichever way the firm finances,
it will not make any difference. How much it borrows
in one market will be irrelevant to the determination
of interest rates and net flows of capital. These depend
only on total supply and demand. If the firm planning to
invest in London borrows in London, this action raises

the interest rate there, and capital flows into Great

Britain. If the same firm had borrowed in New York

to finance its investment in London, then capital would

flow into the United States. The final interest rate and

the net flow of capital will be the same in both cases.

This is true even if the firm is not indifferent to

where it borrows. Suppose arbitrage is not costless;

that is, there are certain costs in bringing a borrower

and lender together. There will then be regularly es-

tablished markets where brokers provide services for

a fee. The firm might get better service in New York,

where it is better known, and so it might finance there.

Or some countries may have no capital market at all;

for example, in the nineteenth century and to some ex-

tent even now, Canadians used the facilities of New

York in lieu of their own capital markets; that is, Cana-

dian borrowers borrowed in New York, while Canadian

lenders lent in New York. But this does not greatly af-

fect world interest rates or the net flows of capital. The

firm chooses to borrow in the financial center where it

gets the best service. By borrowing in this center, the

firm raises the interest rate, and capital flows in from

other centers. The flow of capital between centers en-

sures that interest rates will be identical throughout the

world. The firm's choice of capital market affects the
gross movements of capital but not the net movements
and not the interest rate.

This may be what the world is like. In the nineteenth
century capital appeared to move along channels. There
was specialization—the major capital exporters lent to
certain countries and certain industries. This shows
up in the gross figures, but it might not have been important in explaining net movements. It is not that we
should overlook the importance of the gross figures,
for the use of the facilities in London is a saving to
the Commonwealth countries. It is just that the effect
of gross movements on the international allocation of
resources may be different from the obvious one.

This makes empirical investigation very difficult.
Suppose interest rates are low in London and New York
but high in India and Brazil. To equalize interest rates,
capital must flow out of the first two countries and into
the second two. But even if there are only slight advantages to specialization, it may be that the United States
lends to Brazil and not to India while England lends to
India and not to Brazil. If this is not sufficient to bring
about equality in interest rates, the United States might
lend some to India or lend to England, which in turn

would lend to India. The result may be equilibrium,
but the regression analysis will show that capital flows
between London and Brazil are not sensitive to differences in interest rates between these two countries.
There are two ways of getting around this. If you still
want to use capital flows between two countries as independent variables, then you must make them a function not merely of interest rates but of all other capital
flows. In other words, the flow from London to Brazil
depends on differences in interest rates and on the
amount that the United States lends to Brazil. This
means that you will have more explanatory variables
than independent variables, and since the number of
years in which data are available are very few, statistical investigation is almost impossible.

The other method would be to use net inflows or outflows for each country as the independent variable,
that is, ignore how much goes where and use interest
rates in all other countries as independent variables.
But now let us return to the main theme.

It was important to go through this simple analysis
in detail in order to make certain exactly what we are
trying to explain. We observe in the world a large volume of direct investment. If we wish to know the effects

on interest rates and if markets are perfect, the gross
flows would, for the most part, be irrelevant. It is the
net flows which would be important.

As was pointed out in the introductory chapter, there
do in fact exist cross movements, and Europe's investments in the United States in direct plus portfolio equal
America's investments in Europe in direct plus portfolio. We must, therefore, be careful in interpreting
the meaning of the empirical results. Now we introduce
imperfections which make the gross flows important.

Barriers to Capital Movement

Let us drop the assumption that there are no barriers
to movement between countries. There certainly are
barriers—costs are high, information is poor, and
there is always the risk of exchange-rate changes.
Under these conditions, interest rates do not have to
be equal for equilibrium to exist. They can differ by
the cost of movement. Capital will flow only when the
interest rates differ by more than the costs of movement.

In this model, gross movements are important. If
the firm borrows in London, the interest rate in London
will rise as before, but this will not necessarily bring
forth a flow of capital into Great Britain.

Not only are gross flows important, but the question
of where the firm finances is meaningful, for now interest rates can differ from country to country. But
this does not mean that the firm always borrows in the
country where interest rates are lowest. On the contrary, under certain plausible conditions, the firm will
always find the cost of capital lower in the country
where it is making the investment; that is, any firm in
any country, investing in a foreign country, will find
it cheaper to borrow in the foreign country than to borrow in its own for the foreign investment. With refer-
ences to its operations in Holland, Standard Oil will try
to borrow in Holland rather than the United States; with
reference to its operations in the United States, Royal
Dutch Shell will borrow in the United States.

Behind this assertion is the bold assumption that the
barriers to mobility are the same for the firm as for
the capital market. We shall discuss this later; for the
moment, assume that it is true. We are continuing on
the assumption that the only imperfections or impurities in the market are the barriers to mobility. For the
firm to find interest rates more expensive abroad than
at home, the foreign interest rate must exceed the
domestic interest rate by more than the cost of move-

ment. If the cost of movement is the same for the firm as for the capital market, this is impossible. Movements of portfolio capital will always ensure that the interest rate abroad never exceeds the domestic interest rate by more than transport costs. The firm will always find the interest rate abroad properly discounted for costs of movement at the most equal to the domestic rate and never greater. It therefore will tend to borrow abroad, except in the borderline case, where under present assumptions it would be indifferent.

What validity is there in the assumption that barriers are the same for firms as for the capital market? This should be true where exchange-rate risks are involved. The risk should be the same. But it is not clear in two other respects: (1) the fear of irresponsible borrowing is less when you are lending to your subsidiary than when you are lending to a foreign government or to a firm not under your control (it could, on the other hand, be greater because foreign governments may be more hostile in some instances to direct than to portfolio investment); (2) the transaction costs of international finance (especially the cost of information) are less to the firm than to the market because the firm is, so to speak, on the spot. This is especially true for small

transitory fluctuations. A firm like Standard Oil (New
Jersey), with extensive international operations and
with continual international financing, will be able to
afford large-scale research and might find it profitable to arbitrage deviations from equilibrium. But this
really is not at all a clear case. A firm, except when
it is very large, should have no comparative advantage
in financing transactions, whereas financial institutions
and banks should—and banks do have worldwide affiliations. However, there is some truth in the assertion
of a firm's ability to arbitrage. This is indicated by the
fact that unaffiliated Americans make investments in
the foreign operations of American firms. In 1950
United States investment in American-controlled enterprises was $11.8 billion.[1] About 90 percent of this in-
vestment was supplied by the controlling companies.
The other 10 percent ($1.121 billion) was supplied by
American persons unaffiliated with the controlling enterprise. The investment of these unaffiliated persons

[1] This figure and the ones to follow are taken from U.S.
Department of Commerce, Office of Business Economics,
Direct Private Foreign Investments of the United States:
Census of 1950 (Washington: U.S. Government Printing
Office, 1953), pp. 21, 22.

is similar to portfolio investment. This suggests that
American companies with international operations are
able to finance some of their foreign operations in
United States capital markets—something which foreign firms have typically not been able to do in recent
years. But the unaffiliated investment occurs mainly
in Canada. The area distribution is as follows:

Canada	769 million
Latin America	247 million
Europe	34 million
Other	70 million

The fact that the unaffiliated investment is mostly in
Canada, where there is substantial United States portfolio investment suggests that the arbitrage done by
American firms with international operations is, in
fact, limited.

It is important to stress that what we have been discussing applies only to the financing of foreign assets.
With respect to its domestic assets, there is no exchange risk or international transaction cost involved.
But it could be argued that when Standard Oil (New
Jersey), for example, is borrowing in a foreign country, it will get a particularly favorable interest rate
because foreigners wish to invest not in the foreign

subsidiary but in the whole company. But the local investor could have done this by purchasing shares of
Standard Oil in New York. Or maybe he could not, for
there may be government restrictions.

The hypothesis just suggested—namely, that firms
find capital costs cheaper abroad than at home—may
not seem very convincing or very important. Its main
purpose is not to explain why American firms do, in
fact, borrow abroad to some extent to finance their foreign operations. This might be explained by special
circumstances rather than general conditions. What
has to be explained is why firms operating in foreign
countries do not lend abroad. If a firm establishes a
foreign operation and if capital costs are high abroad,
why does it not arbitrage between the two capital markets by lending abroad aside from its operations? In
fact, this does not seem to happen. The foreign operations of firms are restricted typically to special lines
of endeavor similar to the activities they conduct at
home. One seldom finds firms which have subsidiaries
in underdeveloped countries expanding into diverse and
unrelated lines. This type of behavior is consistent
with a theory in which the foreign investment is motivated by the "profit" of controlling a foreign enterprise

and not consistent with a theory in which higher interest rates are the motivating factor. Hence the importance of the hypothesis under discussion about the
influence of barriers to mobility on financing is clear.

If we analyse the hypothesis further, it can also explain why firms do not diversify their foreign investments even when they do not borrow abroad. At first
this seems strange. If a firm does not borrow abroad
for its foreign operations—and Aramco borrows very
little in Saudi Arabia—then one might argue that capital costs must be higher in this foreign country than
in the United States and that Aramco could profitably
go into international banking. But it must be remem-
bered that there are two interest rates involved. One
is the interest rate at which you can borrow, and the
other is the interest rate at which you can lend. The
borrower's interest rate is always higher than the
lender's interest rate, and the difference between the
two is transaction costs. The size of the transaction
costs and the difference in interest rates depend on the
degree of development of the capital market. In well-
developed markets it is very low, but in regions where
capital markets are poorly developed—and a good many
foreign operations take place in such regions—the dif-
ferential is high.

The theory of portfolio investment applies to the lender's interest rates. The equilibrium conditions are that the rate at which a capitalist can lend in a foreign country will not exceed the rate at which he can lend at home, with due allowance for barriers to international mobility. If we assume these barriers to be the same for firms as for the capital market, then we should expect not to find nonfinancial firms lending money abroad. When we are dealing with well-developed economies, the lending and borrowing rates are very close together. Therefore, the same logic which implies that firms will not lend abroad also implies that they will either borrow abroad or be indifferent. But for regions of underdeveloped capital markets, the case may be quite different. Here the borrowing rate may be quite in excess of the lending rate, so much so that it pays a firm to borrow at home for its international operations while at the same time it does not pay it to lend abroad. This is the type of phenomenon which seems to occur, and it most clearly illustrates the difference between direct and portfolio investment.

Other Imperfections

The arguments just given provide an explanation for why companies borrow abroad to finance their interna-

tional operations. But this reasoning would imply that
if the company borrows abroad, it should do so for
all its capital needs and not for just part of them, as
is, in fact, the case. We now turn to the reasons why
companies do not finance 100 percent of their foreign
assets abroad but supply some of the capital themselves. The existence of transaction costs creating a
spread between borrowing and lending rates may be
one of the reasons, although it is certainly not the only
one. The transaction costs will not be the same for all
types of borrowing. We can order different types of
liabilities in ascending order of transaction costs. Certain current liabilities, taxes payable, wages payable,
and accounts payable, involve almost no transaction
costs because the borrower and the lender are in direct
contact through their everyday business activities. The
firm will most certainly take advantage of some of these
opportunities to borrow. (On the other hand, the interest rate on wages, for example, might be very high because workers are poor and do not have access to borrowing. They might accept substantially lower wages if
paid daily rather than monthly.) Next in order of transaction costs would be bank loans; after this come bonds
and equities. In underdeveloped countries the transac-

tion costs on bonds and equities may be extremely high
because of the absence of any local capital market; for
this reason, one would expect to find that firms operating
in these countries rely mostly on current liabilities and
bank loans for whatever financing they do. Because of
increasing transaction costs the firm may not finance
all its needs abroad but may borrow some in its home
country, where its transaction costs are lower.

There are other reasons why firms will not borrow
100 percent of their liabilities abroad on foreigners'
operations. To explain these reasons, we must move
further away from the perfect model with which we began. In particular, we must drop the assumption that,
aside from transaction costs, firms can borrow as
much as they want at a given interest rate; or, what
probably amounts to the same thing, we must drop the
assumption of perfect certainty and the absence of risk.
Dropping this assumption leads to increased interest
costs with increased borrowing and also leads to the
problem of control.

Empirically there is little to justify an assumption
that a firm can borrow as much as it wants at a given
interest rate. The differences in interest rates on first,
second, and third mortgages may be taken as an ex-

ample of rising interest rates. The explanation of rising
interest rates is probably the existence of risk and uncertainty. The probability that a firm will earn $\underline{x}$ dollars on a project is usually much greater than the probability that it will earn 2x dollars. The firm cannot guar-
antee all of its liabilities equally well; therefore, there
is a range of priorities on claims to income by investors
and a concomitant range of riskiness.

The rising rate of interest may affect the firm's decision on how much to borrow in each country. Suppose
the rate on prime loans is equal in both countries. Only
a fraction of the firm's foreign operations will be considered prime loans. On these prime loans the cost is
the same in both countries; but the fraction considered
prime may not be the same in both countries, and the
increase in costs because of increasing risks may be
greater in one country than in the other. One would expect a slower rise in a large capital market than in a
small one; that is, it is easier to borrow $100 million
in New York than in Guatemala. The percentage of his
portfolio that each investor would have to commit to
this particular loan would be greater in Guatemala than
in New York. Therefore, it would be riskier for Guate-
malans than New Yorkers, and the interest rate would

rise more quickly. Obviously, this is important in those cases of international operations where large fixed investments are required. In these ventures only a very small fraction could possibly be financed locally. For these industries the rate of direct investment to total assets will be higher than for other industries lacking this feature.

The connection between control and financing is very important for international operations. For as an entrepreneur's borrowings cover more of his investment, he usually has to give up control. Suppose an entrepreneur undertakes an investment project where the expected annual return is $10 per year and the cost of the investment is $100. If the interest rate is 5 percent per year, the discounted value of the income stream is $200. The entrepreneur, however, would not usually be able to find someone willing to lend $200 in return for the right to the income, for the capitalist would have little security. The entrepreneur, since he has nothing at stake in the enterprise, would have little incentive to use his assets in the best interest of the lender. The lender will therefore want some control. But in direct investment, the very reason for a firm going abroad is to control the enterprise; it finances part of the operation in order to maintain the control.

The entrepreneur, in deciding how much to borrow abroad, must consider not only the interest costs of the borrowing but also the diminution of profits which will result if he gives up some control. For if the entrepreneur borrows the full $200 in our example, his relation to the foreign enterprise would be that of a consultant. It was stressed in Chapters 2 and 3 that in some instances this would be less profitable than controlling the foreign operation. What the firm seeks by making the direct investment is the extra profits resulting from control. In order to obtain this control, it will have to finance part of the enterprise itself.

The extra profit, it may be recalled, came mainly from the substitution of centralized for decentralized decision making. This enabled the entrepreneur to overcome the conflict of interest which arises from competition between the firms in an imperfect market, or the conflict of the use to be made and the price to be charged for the advantage that is to be exploited. In this context it is easy to see why potential local investors will be particularly anxious to acquire control and why the entrepreneur will be reluctant to relinquish it. For example, the entrepreneur might want to control an enterprise in a foreign country because it is a potential competitor of a firm he owns in another country. If he achieves control over both enterprises, then total profits will be increased. But the incremental profits are joint profits, and they cannot be allocated to either enterprise. An investor who participates in only one of the ventures without control can be prevented from acquiring these extra profits, which will be arbitrarily attributed to the other enterprise. He therefore will be reluctant to purchase equity shares in the enterprise but would prefer fixed income securities unless he can acquire control.

This problem comes up most dramatically in cases where vertical integration is involved. The accounting transfer price is arbitrary, and profits can be allocated to either enterprise. Governments of oil-producing areas have realized this to some extent and are requesting a share in the total profits of oil companies, not just the profits on crude oil. The profits on crude oil are arbitrary because of the impurities in the market, which is one of the reasons for international operation. This is just an example. A similar argument will apply in nearly all cases of international operations, since the conflict of interest is an inherent part of in-

ternational operations. It is the conflict of interest
which necessitates the direct investment by foreclosing
the possibility of borrowing 100 percent of the needed
capital from local sources.

It may be helpful to summarize the arguments just
made. The summary might clarify the choice between
licensing and controlling and also the effect of changing
the interest rate in a country on the amount of direct
investment in that country.

We have tried to show that the firm will nearly always find it cheaper to borrow abroad because the basic
interest rate abroad is at most equal to the interest rate
at home plus the costs of the barriers to movement.
However, the firm will not be able to borrow 100 percent of the capital needed and also maintain control because of the rising interest rates brought about by the
increasing transaction costs and increased risk.

The lower the interest rate abroad, the less the borrowing costs and the more profitable the international
operations. This implies that total assets controlled
abroad will be greater, but the amount of direct investment in these assets will typically be less.

In one sense the lower interest rate abroad will increase the amount of direct investment in the country.

The firm always has the opportunity of licensing, that
is, there is a certain amount of revenue the firm can
obtain without any investment. The lower the interest
rate abroad (and the more profitable the operation), the
less likely the firm is to choose a policy of licensing,
and hence the more likely it is that a direct investment
will occur.

We have so far introduced a few major imperfections
in the capital market and analysed their implications
for the amount of capital associated with international
operations. There are numerous other complications
which could also be introduced into the model. Firms
have connections with financial intermediaries in their
own country which they do not at first have abroad. At
the outset of their international operations, they may
rely on their domestic sources until they establish relations with new sources. There are also other factors
which encourage local borrowing. As a consequence of
its foreign operations, a firm may acquire accounts re-
ceivable from local customers. Local banks will probably be more willing to accept these as collateral for
loans than banks will in the firm's home country. Another reason for local borrowing is the fact that there
are limits on how much a firm can borrow in one year.

The marginal cost of capital in the short run to a rapidly expanding firm may be much higher than "the interest rate" in its country. For this reason a firm
which wishes to enter many foreign markets at once
may borrow locally in each market very heavily, even
if this means licensing when control would be preferable. Later the firm may invest more in its foreign
operations and acquire control.

The number of possible imperfections which could
be introduced is very large, but it would be pointless
to continue introducing them. The problem is not so
much a theoretical problem as an empirical one. Since
there is so very little empirical knowledge, it is almost meaningless to discuss the varied possibilities.

Instead, we may use what we have already discussed
to ask the following important question: Does direct investment move from countries where the interest rate
is low to countries where it is high?

Insofar as capital is the advantage which leads to international operations, the answer is yes. But when
other advantages and other motivations for control are
the causal factors of international operations, the answer is "not necessarily." It can easily happen that a
firm in a country where the interest rate is high finds

it profitable to make a direct investment in a country
where the interest rate is low for the purpose of acquiring control of an enterprise in that country. Empirically, this may not occur very often, if there is an
association between low interest rates and advanced
technology. But even when the capital flow associated
with international operations is in the direction of
higher interest rates, it will only partly result in the
most efficient allocation of world resources. For the
amount of capital accompanying international operations is limited basically to the amount needed for control.

The fact that the lower the interest rate abroad, the
more will be borrowed locally, and hence the less direct investment, is (in a weak sense) a movement in
the right direction; that is, the direction of equalizing
interest rates. But against this must be placed the consideration that when interest rates abroad are high, the
firm may resort to licensing, and in this case there is
no investment at all.

APPENDIX TO CHAPTER 5: AN ALTERNATIVE THEORY OF THE FINANCING OF INTERNATIONAL OPERATIONS

We have assumed throughout this study that basically the same considerations apply to foreign as to domestic operations. We have merely applied the theory of the firm to the special problems resulting from international operations, without assuming any new behavioral postulates. All that was changed were the structural conditions.

Not everyone has taken this view. Some have asserted that a firm behaves quite differently with respect to its foreign operations. In fact, they assert that the firm behaves quite irrationally. The most extreme statement of this view is found in Barlow and Wender's study. The following quotations will make their position clear:

United States companies typically prefer to begin operations in a foreign country in a modest fashion with a small dollar investment. They expand the business within the country through reinvestment of local earnings to the greatest extent possible. They regard their foreign earnings much as a man does his winnings at the race track in that they are much more willing to utilize them than fresh dollar capital for additional foreign investment. United States investment almost always has priority over foreign investment for funds available for expansion.[1]

[1] E. R. Barlow and I. T. Wender, Foreign Investment and Taxation (Englewood Cliffs, N.J.: Prentice-Hall, Inc., 1955), p. 161.

Their explanation of how a man regards racetrack

money is as follows:

> A man may have \$1,000 he has won betting on horses
> and a five dollar bill tucked away in his wallet, which
> he brought with him to the track. He will think nothing
> of wagering five dollars or \$10 to \$100 from the profits
> he has made; whereas he might with some reluctance
> spend the five dollar bill he originally brought with him
> to the races. The gambling profits are not really money
> in the opinion of the gambler as long as he continues to
> gamble. In a story by Damon Runyon, a man kept his
> "eating money" in one pocket and his "race track money"
> in another. The race track money was regarded as
> working capital possessed of a quite different value
> from the "eating money."
> Many companies regard the earnings from their for-
> eign activities in much the same way. They are more
> willing to risk them in subsequent expansion abroad
> than fresh capital from the United States.[2]

Barlow and Wender's statement is the clearest. Other

writers have offered a similar behavioral postulate—

that is, a distinction between retained earnings and new

capital—though they have not put their case quite as ex-

plicitly. For example, the following quotation from E.

Penrose, and especially the last phrase, seems to im-

ply something similar to the Barlow and Wender thesis:

> But a preference for expansion through retained
> earnings is becoming increasingly characteristic of

---

[2]Ibid., pp. 165-166.

the modern corporation, and of particular interest
from the point of view of foreign investment is the
situation, especially favored by American firms, in
which the parent company holds all, or nearly all, of
the equity and permits the subsidiary to expand with
its own earnings.[3]

More explicit is Arndt's statement:

The policy of American companies, well exemplified
by General Motors Holden, appears to have been to retain and reinvest almost all profits for the first few
years of a project and then settle down to a 50/50 ratio in their distribution policy.[4]

It is hard to tell exactly what these hypotheses mean.
I interpret them as saying that investment decisions for
foreign operations are based on the actual amount of
profit made abroad. This is in contrast to a rational
model where an investment decision is based on: (1)
expected profits on investment abroad; (2) expected
profits on investment at home; (3) cost of raising new
capital both at home and abroad. In other words, the rational firm, at appropriate intervals, considers worldwide investment opportunities and worldwide sources

[3] E. T. Penrose, "Foreign Investment and the Growth
of the Firm," Economic Journal, LXVI (June 1956),
p. 220.

[4] H. W. Arndt, "Overseas Borrowing—The New Model,"
Economic Record, XXXIII (August 1957), p. 247.

of funds and with this information maximizes total profits. The rational firm does not consider foreign profits
as "racetrack" money. The decision to invest is the
same whether the money is earned (or borrowed) in the
United States or abroad, with the exception, of course,
of the adjustments required by special risks and costs
involved in converting currencies.

The rational and irrational model do, however, come
very close in certain respects. If actual profits are
viewed as an indicator of expected profits, there will
be an association of actual profits and investment; and
if there are special tax laws or exchange restrictions,
which place a high cost on remitting income, decisions
may be different for blocked funds than for new funds.

The idea that reinvested earnings are different from
new borrowings, if true, might be important. Barlow
and Wender use it as one of the elements to justify their
proposals on taxation policy to affect the flow of direct
investment. One of the requisites of a successful plan
is that "it should fit in with the natural tendency of
companies to expand out of foreign earnings."[5] Exactly

[5]Barlow and Wender, Foreign Investment and Taxation, p. 227.

how it should fit in is not clearly specified.

But the treatment of reinvested earnings has another
special implication which, strictly speaking, is not
necessarily implied in the "racetrack" view, but which,
I suspect, has the same foundation. Frequently, ana-
lysts of balance of payments statistics speak of new investments just covering interest (or profit) payment.
In doing this, they usually commit the fallacy of tying
up one item of a balance sheet to another. It is a fallacy because all items are indirectly connected, and
it is not proper to pick out any two for special attach-
ment, unless a particular case of a direct connection
can be made. If new direct investments are associated
with old profits, then such a connection has been made,
and it is important to spell it out exactly. If the irrationality hypothesis is right, then one would almost be
able to assert that new direct investment will never
exceed earnings; if this were true, it would be important.

Also for the same reasons—namely, the view that
retained earnings are second-class money—profitability
of foreign investment is sometimes measured by taking
the ratio of profits in a given year to original investment excluding retained earnings. This is one of the

measures cited by E. T. Penrose, and by this measure
General Motors earned a profit rate of 560 percent in
Australia. This measure of profit appears to have so
little justification that it is hardly appropriate even to
compute it.

The empirical evidence on this topic is presented in
Table 5.1. This table shows the following five items for
industries and areas and for aggregate direct investment: (1) earnings, (2) income receipts, (3) retained
earnings, (4) capital outflow, and (5) changes in investment. The terminology is the Department of Commerce's
and requires some explanation. "Earnings" refers to
total earnings on direct investment. "Income receipts"
refers to dividends and other incomes remitted from
the foreign subsidiaries. "Retained earnings" is the
difference between earnings and income. "Net capital
outflow" refers to the difference between capital outflow and capital inflow. These outflows and inflows are
the changes in investment financed by means other than
retained earnings. "Changes in investment" is the sum
of net capital outflow and retained earning and is equal
to the change of the indebtedness to Americans of their
subsidiaries or affiliates operating abroad.

This method of classification implies a certain theory

Table 5.1 United States Direct Investment: Earnings, Income,
Receipts, Retained Earnings, Capital Outflow, and Change in
Investment by Industry and Area, 1946-1958 (millions of
dollars)

		1946	1947	1948
All industries	Earnings	832	1,239	1,607
	Income receipts	589	869	1,064
All areas	Retained earnings	243	370	543
	Net capital outflow	230	749	721
	Change in investment	473	1,119	1,264
Areas: Canada	Earnings	210	298	395
	Income receipts	134	178	201
	Retained earnings	76	120	194
	Net capital outflow	47	39	88
	Change in investment	123	159	282
Latin America	Earnings	347	521	675
	Income receipts	281	414	488
	Retained earnings	66	107	187
	Net capital outflow	71	457	333
	Change in investment	137	564	520
Western Europe	Earnings	129	160	193
	Income receipts	64	81	93
	Retained earnings	65	79	100
	Net capital outflow	23	46	64
	Change in investment	88	125	164

1949	1950	1951	1952	1953	1954	1955	1956	1957	1958
1,519	1,769	2,244	2,295	2,218	2,364	2,810	3,134	3,330	2,954
1,112	1,294	1,492	1,419	1,442	1,725	1,912	2,160	2,313	2,198
407	475	752	876	776	644	898	974	1,017	755
660	621	528	850	721	664	779	1,839	2,072	1,094
1,067	1,096	1,280	1,726	1,497	1,308	1,677	2,819	3,089	1,849
393	440	417	421	467	469	591	701	641	568
251	294	236	223	208	237	293	341	367	368
142	146	181	199	259	232	298	360	274	200
100	287	240	420	387	385	300	544	584	398
242	433	421	619	646	617	598	904	858	598
475	631	901	902	722	714	870	1,052	1,166	763
377	522	652	599	570	590	678	840	915	627
98	109	249	303	152	125	192	212	251	135
332	40	166	277	117	88	193	612	1,104	288
430	149	415	580	269	213	385	824	1,355	423
203	262	300	303	316	384	474	485	547	532
93	111	119	127	143	186	255	277	311	325
110	151	181	174	173	198	219	208	236	207
36	119	62	-8	51	50	139	456	254	173
146	270	243	166	224	248	358	664	490	380

Table 5.1 United States Direct Investment: Earnings, Income,
Receipts, Retained Earnings, Capital Outflow, and Change in
Investment by Industry and Area, 1946-1958 (millions of
dollars) (continued)

		1946	1947	1948
Areas:				
West European				
Dependencies	Earnings	42	78	115
	Income receipts	20	31	70
	Retained earnings	22	47	45
	Net capital outflow	5	55	71
	Change in investment	27	102	116
Other areas	Earnings	104	182	232
	Income receipts	91	165	212
	Retained earnings	13	17	20
	Net capital outflow	84	152	165
	Change in investment	97	169	185
Industries:				
Mining and				
smelting	Earnings	72	111	135
	Income receipts	64	99	121
	Retained earnings	8	12	14
	Net capital outflow	-6	36	37
	Change in investment	2	48	51
Petroleum	Earnings	234	404	606
	Income receipts	182	302	453
	Retained earnings	52	102	153

1949	1950	1951	1952	1953	1954	1955	1956	1957	1958
132	95	118	154	182	180	206	220	239	n.a.
98	98	109	126	131	141	164	175	205	n.a.
44	-3	9	27	49	39	42	45	34	n.a.
29	14	1	-5	82	-4	-4	35	66	n.a.
73	11	8	22	131	35	38	80	100	n.a.
315	340	508	515	531	622	669	676	737	n.a.
292	269	376	344	390	571	522	527	515	n.a.
23	71	132	172	143	50	147	149	222	n.a.
163	161	59	166	84	145	151	192	64	n.a.
186	232	191	338	227	195	298	341	286	n.a.
112	145	215	204	149	183	276	356	281	219
86	112	159	159	101	154	195	262	220	182
32	33	56	45	48	29	81	89	61	37
51	87	100	278	243	109	48	95	177	184
83	110	156	323	291	138	129	184	238	321
562	629	900	1,015	997	1,029	1,229	1,406	1,623	1,307
490	555	696	677	759	935	1,026	1,148	1,259	1,204
72	74	204	338	238	94	203	258	364	102

Table 5.1 United States Direct Investment: Earnings, Income, Receipts, Retained Earnings, Capital Outflow, and Change in Investment by Industry and Area, 1946-1958 (millions of dollars) (continued)

		1946	1947	1948
Industries:				
Petroleum	Net capital outflow	186	451	448
	Change in investment	238	553	601
Manufacturing	Earnings	305	434	553
	Income receipts	157	234	251
	Retained earnings	148	200	302
	Net capital outflow	36	107	118
	Change in investment	184	307	420
Other industries	Earnings	221	290	313
	Income receipts	186	234	239
	Retained earnings	35	56	74
	Net capital outflow	14	155	118
	Change in investment	49	211	192

Sources: 1946-1949. S. Pizer and F. Cutler, "Foreign Investments and Income," Survey of Current Business, XXXIV (November 1954), p. 6.
1950-1956. U.S. Department of Commerce, Office of Business Economics, Balance of Payments Statistical Supplement (Washington: U.S. Government Printing Office, 1958), pp. 138-151.
1957. S. Pizer and F. Cutler, "Private Foreign Investments Near $37 Billion," Survey of Current Business, XXXVIII (September 1958), p. 15.
1958. S. Pizer and F. Cutler, "Capital Flow to Foreign Countries Slackens," Survey of Current Business, XXXIX (August 1959), p. 25.

1949	1950	1951	1952	1953	1954	1955	1956	1957	1958
448	248	93	248	408	277	369	1,139	1,332	600
520	322	297	586	646	371	572	1,397	1,696	702
566	623	690	644	675	722	823	858	852	873
307	357	331	287	314	346	383	390	461	471
259	226	359	357	361	376	440	468	391	402
16	192	190	211	-53	111	173	268	370	175
275	418	549	568	308	487	613	736	761	577
279	372	438	432	396	436	483	521	574	555
235	270	305	296	267	291	308	361	373	341
44	102	133	136	129	145	175	160	201	214
145	94	145	113	124	168	189	336	192	135
189	196	278	249	253	313	360	496	393	349

of what a direct investment is. This theory is not the
same as the one we presented earlier. Of the five
items, only two of them appear in the annual balance
of payments accounts. Income receipts from abroad
(and not earnings) are treated as credits; and capital
outflow (and not retained earnings) is treated as a debit.
The justification of this procedure is difficult to com-
prehend. It would seem that in the relationship of a
firm to its wholly owned subsidiary, the difference between retained earnings and capital outflow is arbitrary
and inconsequential. However, as was shown before,
there are theories which view the difference between
retained earnings and capital outflow as meaningful,
and apparently the Department of Commerce shares
this view. It should also be noted that investments refer to the United States share of the equity and debt of
the foreign subsidiaries and not to the total assets of
the subsidiary. I would argue that it would be more
appropriate to treat all assets of the foreign subsidiary
as United States investment and to offset this by a lia-
bility for borrowing in the foreign country. This would
more closely approximate the legal status of the assets
as well as the economic facts. As I have tried to point
out in this study, and especially in this chapter, the

theory of international operations is concerned with the
distribution of total assets abroad. It is the desire to
control these assets that induces the direct investment.

The first thing to notice in Table 5.1 is that in the
aggregate, and for every year, total earnings on United
States investments exceed the change in investment,
sometimes substantially and sometimes by only a little.
This is the same as saying that funds remitted from
abroad (income receipts) exceed funds sent abroad (net
capital outflow). The reader may observe that this phenomenon is not true for all countries or for all industries for all years. There is no point in noting the exceptions, since I know of no theory and no data to explain them.

What does this phenomenon signify? It signifies that
if analysis is restricted to income receipts and capital
flows, that is, if other effects of international operation on imports and exports are ignored, international
operations from 1946 to 1958 have provided a net gain
of foreign exchange for the United States. Is this important? It is if there is a connection between the two.
But if there is no connection, why should these two
items be singled out for comparison? There is, of
course, a connection in the sense that if all interna-

tional operations and capital movements were abolished,
both income and capital inflow would disappear from
balance of payments accounts. But this does not mean
that the balance of payments of the United States would
deteriorate. To know whether this would happen, one
would require information on all the effects of international operations. Also, if there is no other connection,
the fact loses much importance because it does not imply that in the future the same phenomenon will again
appear.

We have not yet considered the gambling money thesis.
This thesis argues that there is a certain relationship
between total earnings and retained earnings. However,
as the table shows, this relation varies from industry
to industry and from country to country.[6] Once again I
do not point out these variations because I have no theory to explain them. They may well be caused merely
by accounting procedure. One case, however, is inter-

[6] It also might be noted that in Canada, in the postwar
period, foreign-controlled firms have distributed as
dividends a higher percentage of their income than have
non-foreign-controlled firms. See Dominion Bureau of
Statistics, Canada's International Investment Position
1926-1954 (Ottawa: Queen's Printer and Controller of
Stationery, 1956), pp. 60-61.

esting. It will be seen that in manufacturing, earnings
are divided (very approximately but more so than in
other industries) between income and retained earnings
in about a 50/50 ratio. This is especially interesting
when we compare retained earnings to net capital outflow. Net capital outflow shows very severe drops in
1949, 1953, and 1958—three recession years. These
drops occurred without any drop in foreign earnings
and without any great falloff in retained earnings. This
might be an indication that there is something quite
different about retained earnings (old money) and capital outflow (new money). However, as we show pres-
ently, the difference in behavior could also be explained
without proposing a theoretical difference between the
two types of capital flows.

The distinction between retained earnings and new
borrowings makes sense when you are dealing with the
relation of a firm to the capital market. It does not
make sense when you are dealing with the relation of
a firm to its subsidiary, except as an arbitrary accounting device. Suppose the accounting rules were as
follows:[7]

---

[7]Using the same Department of Commerce definitions
as were used before.

1. Capital outflow is equal to the excess of intended
investment over profits when such an excess exists.
2. Income receipts are equal to the excess of earnings
over the intended change in the amount invested when
such an excess exists and when both are positive.
3. Capital inflow occurs when the firm disinvests and
is equal to the excess of the firm's disinvestment over
its profits.

The principles are illustrated in Table 5.2. In the
table we consider a number of enterprises, each making
$1 profit. The table illustrates the effect on the account-
ing books of various investments ranging from a positive investment of $3 to a disinvestment of $3.

This table indicates for any given investment what
retained earnings, income receipts, and so forth, will
be for foreign enterprises making $1 profit. The es-
sentials would be the same if we considered firms
making various amounts of profit. Suppose we continue with our example and estimate the aggregate
figures. That is, we are assuming that the earnings
of the foreign enterprises are all one dollar, and we
wish to know what the aggregate flows will be when the
decision to invest is changed. Compare two different

Table 5.2 Relationships of Earnings and Capital Flows

	Firms Numbered							Aggregate of Firms	
	1	2	3	4 5	6	7	1-6	2-7
1 Earnings	1	1	1	1 1	1	1	6	6
2 Change in investment	+3	+2	+1	0 -1	-2	-3	+3	-3
3 Income receipts	0	0	0	1 1	1	1	3	4
4 Retained earnings	1	1	1	0 0	0	0	3	2
5 Capital outflow	2	1	0	0 0	0	0	3	1
6 Capital inflow	0	0	0	0 -1	-2	-3	-3	-6
7 Net capital flow 5 + 6	2	1	0	0 -1	-2	-3	0	-5

cases: in both six enterprises are involved, each makes
$1 profit, and aggregate profits are therefore $6. In
Case 1, entrepreneurs are prone to invest abroad. The
largest investor plans to invest $3, the next one $2,
and so on, until the sixth investor, who plans to disin-
vest $2. In this case columns 1 to 6 apply, and aggre-
gate investment, as shown in column 8 of the table, is
$3. In Case 2, the entrepreneurs are wary of foreign
operations, and each entrepreneur decides to invest one

dollar less than in the previous case. Now the largest
investor invests $2 rather than $3, and the smallest
disinvests $3 rather than $2. Columns 2 to 7 apply,
and aggregate investment is now minus $3, a change
of $6.

Look at retained earnings and net capital outflow.
Retained earnings have shifted from $3 to $2, a change
of only $1. But net capital outflow has shifted from 0
to $5, a change of -$5. This is similar to the type of
behavior we observed earlier in the time series of
American direct investment. Yet it occurs without regard to any 50 percent rule or any other nontrivial rule
relating income, retained earnings, and investment. It
is caused by purely arbitrary accounting devices. This,
I suggest, is an equally plausible interpretation of the
data. Of course, it does not disprove the "racetrack"
(or 50/50) rule. I am not sure that a rule based on so
little theory needs disproving. However, before leaving the subject, I should make it clear that I do not in
any sense mean to imply by this brief treatment that
there is nothing worth studying in the dynamics of financing international operations. There certainly is,
but I have nothing useful to suggest.

6

EFFECTS OF INTERNATIONAL OPERATIONS ON INCOME

It is almost impossible to evaluate the effects of international operations on world income and its distribution among countries. A direct investment changes production possibilities, income distribution, and prices. There are difficult theoretical problems in evaluating these changes, and our knowledge of empirical conditions is almost nil. All we attempt to do in this chapter is to illustrate certain facets of the problem which arise directly out of the analysis we have presented. It is important to stress that these are merely isolated partial-equilibrium considerations. By themselves, they provide no guide for policy; in a broader theory which may someday be developed, they may be useful.

The analysis is based on four aspects of international operations: (1) the capital usually associated with international operations, (2) the advantages or technical knowledge sometimes associated, (3) the fact of centralized rather than decentralized control, and (4) the nationality of the controller.

Since most of the points made have already been discussed in earlier chapters, we shall at times be brief.

Associated Capital Movements
We begin with the associated capital movements, because this aspect has traditionally received the most

attention and not because it is necessarily the most important feature. In fact, a case could be made that it
has received too much attention. It certainly causes a
great deal of trouble.

Some of the hostility to direct investments, especially
in underdeveloped countries, is a psychological hostility
to foreign "capital," hostility which neglects the other
equally important side of international operations, en-
trepreneurship. The international flow of managerial
and entrepreneurial skills might be greatly increased
if there was not the fear of expropriation generated by
this hostility. The economics might not be changed,
but the suggestion is made that international operations
would be psychologically more palatable to underdeveloped nations if a new form were used on the theme
of the management contract—a form where capital is
not involved. It is not easy to find an acceptable form
because the motivation of the capital movement is control, and the new form must somehow also solve the
conflicts of interest discussed in Chapter 2. And the
real cause of hostility may be the control, even though
the hostility is now directed against the form. But
some feasible forms may be developed.

The beneficial effects of direct investment on the allocation of the world's capital are limited. The motivation for the movement is generally control, not interest differentials. The amount of capital that moves is therefore limited, and it may move in the wrong direction, that is, to places where the interest rate is low. To some extent, the lower the interest rate abroad, the more the capital flow or, in any case, the greater the number and the larger the size of international operations. For the lower the interest rate abroad, the more local borrowing is possible, and the more profitable the operations are. If local borrowing is not possible, the investment may not even occur. The firm may choose instead to license. For this and other reasons, it is usually inappropriate to consider direct investment as a substitute for portfolio investment in the task of allocating the world's capital.

An increase in direct investment is sometimes suggested as a means of solving balance of payments difficulties. This brings up transfer problems, both the "transfer in" problem, when the investment is made, and the "transfer out" problem, when dividend payments are made or capital is repatriated.

First, let us consider the "transfer in" problem. Does the establishment of an international operation

generate an increase in demand for imports greater
than, equal to, or less than the supply of foreign exchange resulting from the associated capital flow? The
analysis of this problem is very complex. We shall restrict ourselves to a few points. It is nearly always
certain that the amount of new investment generated
by the international operation exceeds the capital inflow. This is so for two reasons. First, companies
typically borrow some of the capital needed for their
operations from local sources in the country where they
are establishing the enterprise. Second, there are ac-
celerator effects. The establishment of the enterprise
leads directly to increases in the demand for other commodities, and investment by natives is required to produce these commodities. The fact that the investment
exceeds the capital inflow tells us only a little about
the effect on the balance of payments. What happens to
imports depends on the income generated by the investment and on the marginal propensity to import. About
these, little can be said in general except to point out
that the propensity to import of a direct investment is
probably higher than for the economy as a whole. In
fact, it often happens that the amount of direct investment is exactly equal to the amount of imports directly

associated with the international operations. This happens, for example, when a company provides technical knowledge in return for an equity interest and the enterprise is otherwise financed locally. The company in this case furnishes capital in the form of the discounted value of the productivity of its technique, but the capital furnished exactly equals the import, and no free foreign exchange is provided.

The "transfer out" problem applies not only to dividends and repatriation payments but also to royalty and rental payments. In fact, it applies to all payments for all imports. The problem is basically one of giving up resources for the imported service or good, and it does not matter much which particular service or good you are paying for. The difficulty of paying for what you buy is common to all; the important question is: Do you get more than you pay for? In particular, the question boils down to this: Does the increase in income in a country resulting from international operations exceed what it must pay for these operations in terms of rents, royalties, interest, and profit? A little later we shall touch lightly upon this problem, but the situation is really too complex to handle with our present knowledge.

But even if the increase in income exceeds the costs,
there is another meaning to the transfer problem which
is relevant. This basically involves a question of timing.
There is a certain cost associated with moving along
the production-possibilities curve and changing from
a surplus balance of trade to a deficit. This cost is far
greater if the adjustment is made in a short period of
time than if it is made gradually. It therefore makes
quite a difference if there is some force at work which
causes the repayments to cluster in a short period.
The crisis caused by a simultaneous decision on the
part of a large number of creditors to take their money
out can be quite severe.

The important question is whether such a clustering
is likely to occur. This seems to be the real significance
of the compound interest games one encounters so often.
If new investment each year exactly equals service payments on old investment, aggregate investment will
grow at the compound interest rate. This, as is most
familiar, is an exponential equation, and it goes up
very quickly. But no matter how impressive the rise,
the percentage change at each and every point is still
only the interest rate. The decision for a country each
year (if countries can and do make such decisions) is

the same: if the interest rate is 3 percent, the question
is whether the productivity that would be lost by re-
patriating the loan does or does not exceed the 3 percent; if it is more than 3 percent, then it certainly
pays to "borrow the interest." The decision is exactly
the same at all points, and the fact of exponential growth
is irrelevant.

What may be relevant is the possibility that a crisis
will occur which will force the country to pay back all
its borrowings at one time. This can be costly (though
often the burden is shifted by the borrower to the lender). Such a crisis did develop in the thirties, though
significantly it was more important for portfolio investment than for direct investment. (To repatriate a
direct investment, you must sell the enterprise; in
times of crisis you usually cannot get very much for
it, and if you do find a buyer, his purchase helps to
decrease internal spending and thus facilitates the
transfer.) Not much can be said about whether international operations are subject to violent fluctuations
because we know so little about the mechanisms involved. Probably it is a fruitful area of research.

Associated Technical Knowledge

Usually ability and technique accompany international

operations. But it is not a necessary condition. The
motive of control may be the removal of conflict between enterprises which sell in the same market or
which deal with each other. Or the motive may be diversification. The firm making the direct investment
need not have any advantage; all that is required is
market impurity in the first case and negative covari-
ance in the income of enterprises of different countries
in the second case.

Where an advantage is involved, the important question is: How much does it cost, relative to what it is
worth? The cost may very well exceed its value if, for
example, consumer's tastes are not considered a legiti-
mate criterion of worth. Aside from this, competition
provides a check on the amount the firm receives for
its advantage. In the long run, it can get no more than
the difference between its ability and the ability of other
firms. But this is not the complete case, for there are
problems of change in advantages through time. Does
an enterprise increase its advantage through time because of its gain in experience and in consumers' ac-
ceptance? Or does the firm lose its advantage because
of the demonstration effect and the consequent attrac-
tion of new competitors? In some cases one happens,

and in some cases the other. What the net effect of international operation may be is not known. But in cases
where the advantages increase through time (and the
profitability of the firm along with them), there may be
an infant-firm argument for subsidizing a local company. This may be the rationale of the policy of some
countries to enforce a greater recruitment of local
personnel than the company desires.

The receiving country is interested in knowing not
only whether the benefits are less than costs but also
whether the costs are as low as they can be. The significant aspect of most advantages is that marginal
costs are close to zero. They are certainly less than
the price paid for them. There is no, or little, marginal cost in utilizing a patent, or information, or a
brand name, or most other advantages one could name.
In most cases the price paid for the advantage, though
less than the benefit derived from them, is greater
than the cost of the advantage. There is room for bargaining, and the study of this bargaining relation is
fascinating; but we have little to add on this subject.

The Fact of Centralized Control

The fact that two enterprises in different countries are
controlled by the same firm sometimes leads to a situ-

ation closer to marginal-cost pricing and sometimes farther away.

In the case of horizontal integration, the difference between price and marginal cost will most likely be greater when there is centralized control than decentralized. If the rest of the world were perfectly competitive, this would mean decrease in world welfare. Since there are, in fact, monopoly elements everywhere, the effect of monopoly pricing in one part of an industry is unknown. As to how the gains and losses of monopoly control are distributed between countries, the best answer is that it depends; I do not think that there is a general presumption one way or the other.

Vertical integration presents quite a different aspect. Here the motivation of control is to solve a bilateral-monopoly problem. This is of importance only where sequential monopoly is involved. The removal of sequential monopoly results in a closer approximation to marginal-cost pricing.

Here a little more can be said about the distribution of the gains. Suppose Country A produces and entirely exports a raw material which is processed further and sold to consumers in Country B. If the industry is monopolistic in both countries, then vertical integration will benefit consumers in Country B by lowering prices. The firm will also benefit because total profits will be greater. Country A will enjoy an increase of production in its commodity, but its total revenue may fall or rise depending on what share it receives of the profits of the new, vertically integrated firm.

The fact of centralized control may lead to an improvement in the worldwide use of resources in a sense quite different from the one just discussed. The connection between markets is often quite imperfect. The international operations may serve to integrate previously remote markets. A firm operating in many countries may be expected to react more quickly to changing conditions in a particular country, that is, more quickly than the market. This is because of the better communications within a firm.

This may particularly affect the international flow of capital and the transmission of business cycles. As we saw in Chapter 4, American foreign investment was sensitive to American business cycles. This is because the firm is subject to worldwide influences on its sources and uses of funds. For the same reason, of course, the United States is more sensitive to foreign business cycles. The sensitivity depends not primarily on the fact

of international operations. Greater interdependence
is precisely what to expect for greater integration; it
is the price paid for it, and it is probably what makes
integration of nations difficult to achieve.

The existence of international operations may change
tariff policy of some countries, and this brings up the
question of the nationality of the firm.

The Nationality of the Firm

It is fitting to end this chapter and the study on the subject of the nationality of the firm. For this has been an
important element in all our analyses. Is the behavior
of the firm affected by its nationality? In general, one
would expect not. Firms are firms; they maximize
profits and therefore should behave roughly the same
way. But there are important exceptions, and basically
they stem from the risks of operating in a foreign country, although there are other things as well.

Since the shareholders of an American firm expect
to be paid in dollars, the firm must worry about converting its foreign profits into dollars. This will affect its behavior. For example, it will tend to keep its
liquid assets in its own country. On any particular aspect of its enterprise—for example, research labs or
head offices—if the costs are the same in both coun-

tries, or almost the same, the firm will choose to lo-
cate at home or abroad.

The selection of its personnel may be biased. If a
firm is hiring potential executives, it will reasonably
expect that someday it will wish to bring the employee
to its head office. If the prospective applicant is a foreigner who will not or cannot give up his citizenship or
residence, he is less likely to be acceptable than a national.

The nationality of the firm may also affect capital
flows. Suppose that in each capital market there is a
bias against lending to foreigners. If this is true, then,
for example, the American owners of an American firm
will view the opportunity cost of their investment as the
profit they could earn by investing in another American
firm. Consider a firm with operations in Canada and
the United States, and suppose that the Canadian activities become unprofitable and it is decided to liquidate
the enterprise. It may be that because of bias in the
capital market, the place where the capital will be trans-
ferred to will be influenced not only by profit considerations but by nationality. If citizens of the United States
own the firm, the money will be invested in a United
States firm. If citizens of Canada own the firm, the

money might be invested in a Canadian firm. How true
this will be and how important depend on the nature and
extent of imperfections in the capital market, about
which we know little.

Finally, there is the effect on tariffs. If a United
States industry is "threatened" by cheap foreign imports, the reaction of firms in the industry will be quite
different if these firms have international operations.
We can see this quite clearly in tariff debates at present.
In some industries some of the firms operate abroad,
while others do not. When a tariff is proposed, the difference in attitudes of the two kinds of firms is striking. However, this is a simplification; the interests of
a firm in a tariff are more complex than that, and a
firm like Singer, with extensive international operations, will complain about Japanese imports. But on
the whole, international operations tend to make firms
free traders. In the absence of international operations,
firms are either gainers from exports or losers from
imports (or neither), and this affects their stand on free
trade. But a firm with international operations is in
both positions at the same time.

This is a hopeful note to end on for those who look
forward to an integrated world economy. The fact of

having international operations may lead firms to become international rather than national.

SELECTED BIBLIOGRAPHY

Books

Bain, Joe S. Barriers to New Competition. Cambridge, Mass.: Harvard University Press, 1956.

Barlow, E. R., and Wender, I. T. Foreign Investment and Taxation. Englewood Cliffs, N. J.: Prentice-Hall, Inc., 1955.

Brazil—Factors Affecting Foreign Investment. Menlo Park, Calif.: Stanford Research Institute, 1955.

Brecher, I., and Reisman, S. S. Canada-United States Economic Relations. Ottawa: Royal Commission on Canada's Economic Prospects, 1957.

Corey, L. Meat and Man. New York: The Viking Press, 1950.

Dunning, John H. American Investment in British Manufacturing Industry. London: George Allen and Unwin Ltd., 1958.

Iversen, Carl. Some Aspects of the Theory of International Capital Movements. Copenhagen: Einer Munksgaard, 1935.

Kindleberger, C. P. International Economics, 2d. ed. Homewood, Ill.: Richard D. Irwin, Inc., 1958.

Lewis, C. America's Stake in International Investments. Washington: Brookings Institution, 1938.

Markham, J. W. Competition in the Rayon Industry. Cambridge, Mass.: Harvard University Press, 1952.

Marshall, H., Southard, F. A., and Taylor, K.
Canadian-American Industry. New Haven: Yale University Press, 1936.

Phelps, D. M., Migration of Industry to South America.
New York: McGraw-Hill Book Company, Inc., 1936.

Southard, F. A. American Industry in Europe. Boston:
Houghton Mifflin Company, 1931.

Articles

Arndt, T. W. "Overseas Borrowing—the New Model,"
Economic Record, XXXIII (August 1957), p. 24.

Block, Ernest. "United States Foreign Investment and
Dollar Shortage," The Review of Economics and Statistics, XXXV (May 1953), p. 154.

Blyth, C. D., and Canty, E. B. "Non-Resident Ownership of Canadian Industries," Canadian Journal of Economics and Political Science, XXII (November 1958),
p. 449.

Penrose, E. T. "Foreign Investment and the Growth
of the Firm," Economic Journal, LXVI (June 1956),
p. 220.

———. "Profit Sharing Between Producing Countries
and Oil Companies in the Middle East," Economic
Journal, LXIX (June 1959), p. 238.

Pizer, S., and Cutler, F. "Foreign Investments and
Income," Survey of Current Business, XXXIV
(November 1954), p. 6.

———. "Growth of Foreign Investments in the United States and Abroad," Survey of Current Business, XXXVI (August 1956), p. 14.

———. "Private Foreign Investments Near $37 Billion," Survey of Current Business, XXXVIII (September 1958), p. 15.

———. "Capital Flow to Foreign Countries Slackens," Survey of Current Business, XXXIX (August 1959), p. 25.

Smith, J. E. "U.S. Firms Conduct Lively Technical Exchanges with Foreign Companies," Foreign Commerce Weekly, December 29, 1958.

Wu, Y. "International Capital Investment and the Development of Poor Countries," Economic Journal, LVI (March 1946).

United States Government Publications

Department of Commerce. Direct Private Foreign Investments of the United States, Census of 1950. Washington: U.S. Government Printing Office, 1953.

———. Factors Limiting U.S. Investments Abroad. Part 2, Businessmen's Views on the U.S. Government's Role. Washington: U.S. Government Printing Office, 1954.

———. U.S. Investments in the Latin American Economy. Washington: U.S. Government Printing Office, 1957.

————. Balance of Payments Statistical Supplement.
Washington: U.S. Government Printing Office, 1958.

Federal Trade Commission. Report of the Federal
Trade Commission on Industrial Concentration and
Product Diversification in the 1,000 Largest Manufacturing Companies: 1950. Washington: U.S. Government Printing Office, 1957.

Internal Revenue Service. Statistics of Income, Part II.
Washington: U.S. Government Printing Office, annual
issue.

Government of Canada Publications

Dominion Bureau of Statistics. Canada's International
Investment Position 1926-1954. Ottawa: Queen's Printer
and Controller of Stationery, 1958.

Other Sources

Annual reports of selected United States manufacturing companies.

CURRICULUM VITAE

Stephen Herbert Hymer

Vital Statistics
Born: November 15, 1934, Montreal, Canada
Marital Status: Married, two sons

Academic Background
McGill University, B.A., 1955 (first-class honors in
  economics and political science)
Massachusetts Institute of Technology, Ph.D., 1960

Summary of Career
Teaching Assistant and Instructor, M.I.T., 1957-1959
Lecturer, University College of Ghana, 1960-1961
Assistant Professor, M.I.T., 1961-1962
Assistant Professor, Yale University, 1962-1966
Visiting Research Associate, University of Ghana,
  on leave from Yale, 1963-1964
Associate Professor, Yale University, 1966
Member of the Canadian Government Task Force on
  the Structure of Canadian Industry, 1967
Academic Visitor, The London School of Economics,
  Fall 1969
Visiting Professor, University of Toronto (Series of
  Lectures on African Development), January 1969
Visiting Research Fellow, Institute of Social and
  Economic Studies, University of the West Indies,
  St. Augustine, Trinidad, Spring 1969
Profesore/Investigador, Instituto de Estudios Inter-
  nacionale, Universidad de Chile, Summer 1969
Professor of Economics, The Graduate Faculty, The
  New School for Social Research, 1970-1974
Editor, American Economic Review, January 1974

PUBLICATIONS AND RESEARCH

Stephen Herbert Hymer

1 "The International Operations of National Firms: A Study of Direct Foreign Investment," Unpublished Doctoral Dissertation, Massachusetts Institute of Technology, June 1960.

2 "Turnover of Firms as a Measure of Market Behavior," Review of Economics and Statistics, Vol. XLIV, No. 1 (February 1962), with B. P. Pashigian.

3 "Firm Size and Rate of Growth," The Journal of Political Economy, Vol. LXX, No. 6 (December 1962), with B. P. Pashigian.

4 "Reply: Firm Size and Rate of Growth," The Journal of Political Economy, Vol. LXXII, No. 1 (February 1964), with B. P. Pashigian.

5 "Investment in the Ghana Cocoa Industry: Some Problems of Structure and Policy," The Economic Bulletin, Vol. IX, No. 1 (1965), with R. H. Green.

6 "Comments on the Transfer of Technical Knowledge by International Corporations to Developing Economies," Papers and Proceedings of the American Economic Association, May 1966.

7 "Antitrust and American Investment Abroad," International Aspects of Antitrust, Hearings before the Subcommittee on Antitrust and Monopoly of the Committee on the Judiciary, United States Senate, Eighty-Ninth Congress: Second Session, April 20, 1966.

8 "Cocoa in the Gold Coast: A Study in the Relations Between African Farmers and Agricultural Experts,"

The Journal of Economic History, Vol. XXVI, No. 3
(September 1966), with R. H. Green.

9 "Direct Foreign Investment and the National Interest," in Peter Russell, ed., Nationalism in Canada
(Toronto: McGraw-Hill, 1966).

10 Review of The Teaching of Development Economics,
Kurt Martin and John Knapp, eds. (Chicago: Aldine
Publishing Company, 1967), The Journal of Finance,
Fall 1968.

11 "The Multinational Corporation and the Nation
State," Outline and Reference Bibliography, January
1968.

12 "Canadian Independence and a Choice for the Third
World," in Stephen Clarkson, ed., An Independent
Foreign Policy for Canada (Toronto: McClelland and
Stewart Ltd., 1968), with Brian Van Arkadie.

13 "The Impact of the Multinational Firm," in M. Byé,
ed., La Politique Industrielle de l'Europe Intégrée et
L'Apport des Capitaux Extérieurs (Paris: Presses
Universitaires de France, 1968).

14 "The Multinational Corporation: An Analysis of
Some Motives for International Business Integration,"
Revue Economique, Vol. XIX, No. 6 (November 1968).

15 "A Model of the Agrarian Economy Including Non-
Agricultural Activities," American Economic Review,
September 1969.

16 "Interactions Between the Government and the
Private Sector in Underdeveloped Countries: Govern-

ment Expenditure Policy and the Reflection Ratio," in
Ian Stewart, ed., Economic Development and Structural Change (Edinburgh: Edinburgh University Press,
1969). Published in French as "Les Interactions entre
le Gouvernement et le Secteur Privé," l'Actualité
Economique, No. 3 (Octobre-Decembre, 1968).

17 "A Note on the Capacity to Transform and the Wel-
fare Costs of Fluctuations in the Terms of Trade,"
Economic Journal, December 1969, with R. Albert
Berry.

18 "National Policies Towards Multinational Corporations," A Report for the Task Force on Foreign Ownership and the Structure of Canadian Industry (Ottawa:
Queen's Printer and Controller of Stationery, 1969).

19 "Comments on Public and Private Enterprise in
Africa" in G. Ranis, ed., Government and Economic
Development (New Haven: Yale University Press,
1969).

20 "Multinational Corporations and International Oligopoly: The Non-American Challenge," in C. P. Kindleberger, ed., The International Corporation (Cambridge,
Mass.: The M.I.T. Press, 1970), with R. Rowthorn.

21 "The Efficiency (Contradictions) of the Multinational Corporation," Papers and Proceedings of the
American Economic Association, May 1970.

22 "Capital and Capitalists," Foreword to Polly Hill,
Studies in Rural Capitalism in West Africa (Cambridge:
Cambridge University Press, 1970).

23 "Economic Forms in Pre-Colonial Ghana," Journal of Economic History, June 1970.

24 "The Political Economy of the Gold Coast and Ghana," in G. Ranis, ed., Government and Economic Development (New Haven: Yale University Press, 1970).

25 "The Crisis and Drama of the Global Partnership," The International Journal, Winter 1969-1970, with Stephen Resnick.

26 "International Trade and Uneven Development," in J. W. Bhagwati, R. W. Jones, R. A. Mundell, and Jaroslav Vanek, eds., Trade, Balance of Payments and Growth (Amsterdam: North Holland Publishing Company, 1971), with Stephen Resnick.

27 Statement on The Multinational Corporation and International Investment. Hearing before the Subcommittee on Foreign Economic Policy of the Joint Economic Committee, Ninety-First Congress, Second Session, July 30, 1970.

28 International Big Business 1957-1967 (Cambridge: Cambridge University Press, 1970), by R. Rowthorn in collaboration with S. Hymer.

29 "The Multinational Corporation and the Law of Uneven Development," J. W. Bhagwati, ed., Economics and World Order (New York: World Law Fund, 1971).

30 "Robinson Crusoe and the Secret of Primitive Accumulation," Monthly Review, September 1971.

31 "Partners in Development: The Multinational Corporation and Its Allies," Newstatements, Vol. I, No. 1
(1971).

32 "The Internationalization of Capital," The Journal
of Economic Issues, March 1972.

33 "Statistical Abstract" in G. B. Kay, ed., The
Political Economy of Colonialism in Ghana" (Cambridge:
Cambridge University Press, 1972), in collaboration
with G. B. Kay.

34 "The United States Multinational Corporation and
Japanese Competition in the Pacific," Chuokoron-sha,
Spring 1972.

35 "Some Empirical Facts about U.S. Investment
Abroad," in P. Drysdale, ed., Direct Foreign Invest-
ment in Asia and the Pacific (Canberra: Australian
National University Press, 1972).

36 "The Political Economy of the New Left," Quarterly
Journal of Economics, November 1972, with Frank
Roosevelt.

37 "Is the Multinational Corporation Doomed?"
Innovation, No. 28 (1972).

38 "The Multinational Corporation: Your Home Is Our
Home," Canadian Dimension, March/April 1972.

39 "On Tinkering with Takeovers and Leaving Capitalism to Flourish," Canadian Dimension, June 1972.

40 "Multinationale Konzerne und das Gesetz der un-
gleichen Entwicklung" in Dieter Senghaas, ed., Im-

perialismus and Strukturelle Gewalt: Analysen ueber
abhaengige Reproduktion (Frankfurt: Suhrkamp Ver-
lag, 1972).

41 Notes on the United Nations Report on International
Corporations in World Development. Testimony before
the group of eminent persons to study the impact of
multinational corporations on development and on international relations. Geneva: United Nations, November 6, 1973.

42 "International Economics and International Politics:
A Radical Approach," prepared for a Brookings Institute Volume on the International Economy, January
1974.

43 Spanish, Italian, and Japanese editions of Essays
on the Multinational Corporation.

INDEX

Abbott Laboratories, 113
Advantages, 92, 211
  of American firms, 168
  change in, 218
  cost, 44
  international distribu-
    tion of, 72-85
  and marginal costs, 219
  and movement of direct
    investment, 190
  of national firms, 34
  possession of, 41-46
  product differentiation,
    44
Advertising, 45
Agricultural equipment
  industry, in U.K.,
    142
Allied Chemical and Dye,
    113
Allis-Chalmers Manu-
  facturing Co., 116
Allocation
  of world's capital, 212-
    213
  See also Distribution
Aluminum plants, 40
American Can Co., 115
American Home Products
  Corp., 113
American Radiator and
  Standard Sanitary
  Corp., 115
American Radiator Co.,
  in Europe, 149
American Viscose, 79

Antitrust
  politics of, 86
  See also Monopoly
Apparel industry, foreign
  investment of, 107
Argentina
  foreign investment in,
    109
  industrial distribution
    in, 162
  U.S. sales in, 158
  See also Latin America
Armco Steel Corp., 115
Armour and Co., 109
Arndt, H. W., 194
Attitudes, toward foreign
  investment, 24, 86,
    192, 212
Australia, 78n
  licensing in, 56-57, 62
  national income of, 77
  U.S. direct investment
    in, 77
Automobile industry
  cross investment in, 121
  foreign investment in,
    110-112
  in Latin America, 156
  See also Motor vehicles
    industry

Bain, J. S., 42, 44-45
Balance of payments, 83,
  206, 214
  and new investments,
    196